Exploring New York's
SoHo

Alfred Pommer & Eleanor Winters

Watercolors by Leendert van der Pool

THE
History
PRESS

Published by The History Press
Charleston, SC 29403
www.historypress.net

Cover paintings by Leendert van der Pool. *Front*: Little Singer Building.
Back: Haughwout Building (left) and statue of Puck on the Puck Building.

All photos that are not otherwise credited are by Alfred Pommer.
Maps are drawn by Eleanor Winters.

First published 2012

ISBN 978.1.5402.3154.3

Library of Congress CIP data applied for.

For Joyce and Leendert, with love.

CONTENTS

CONTENTS

ACKNOWLEDGEMENTS

The authors would like to thank Fran Leadon and the *AIA Guide to New York City*, an invaluable resource for New Yorkers and visitors to the city. We are particularly grateful to Mr. Leadon for allowing us to quote freely from his book and for offering us additional advice and information. We would also like to thank John Grafton of Dover Publications, Inc., for granting us permission to reproduce material from Dover books, including his own book, *New York in the Nineteenth Century* (1977), an excellent source of illustration and historical material.

We would also like to express our gratitude to our editor, Whitney Tarella, whose expertise and generosity of spirit has made working with her a pleasure. Thanks are also due to Robert Cooperman, poet and author, whose knowledge of grammar and syntax and eye for the "infelicitous phrase" has saved us on more than one occasion.

INTRODUCTION

New York's SoHo (as opposed to London's Soho, with a lower-case *h*) is a neighborhood in Manhattan that is familiar to tourists from all parts of the globe. What do they think of when they hear the word "SoHo?" The answer might be: "SoHo? Artists in big lofts!" "SoHo? Shopping!" or, very possibly, "SoHo? Cast-iron architecture!"

But what if we told you that SoHo at one time—before it was called SoHo—was the center of New York's show business world, a neighborhood of theaters, spectacles and pleasure gardens? What if we told you that, in the nineteenth century, the SoHo red-light district was so famous (OK, infamous) that guide books were published listing the best brothels in the neighborhood? And shopping? One hundred years before the up-market brand-name boutiques arrived, SoHo's streets were lined with the biggest shopping emporia in the world, multi-story retail palaces selling just about everything one could imagine. George Washington may not have slept here (actually he did, pretty close by), but Mary Todd Lincoln shopped here!

And who walked these streets? The richest and the poorest, John Jacob Astor and Harry Houdini, Aaron Burr and Cornelius Vanderbilt, P.T. Barnum and the Girl in the Red Velvet Swing. We have tales to tell of these and many other larger-than-life personalities who lived, worked or haunted these streets.

Let's stop for a moment and answer a couple of important questions: What exactly is SoHo? And where is it?

SoHo, as many of you know, stands for South of Houston Street, Houston Street being an east–west thoroughfare that neatly cuts across Manhattan Island. North of Houston Street lies Greenwich Village. SoHo was so named in the 1960s when a number of artists "discovered" the area, which at the time was at a particularly low ebb in its erratic history. In fact, SoHo has had a singularly uneven history, as far as popularity, desirability and trendiness (or lack thereof) are concerned. It is a neighborhood that has risen and fallen more than once, redefining itself in some remarkable ways over the years. We'll have a lot more to say about this later.

The boundaries of SoHo were designated by the New York City Landmarks Preservation Commission in 1973 to include a roughly rectangular area from Canal Street on the south to Houston Street on the north, Crosby Street on the east and West Broadway on the west. These, however, are just the boundaries of the so-called SoHo Cast-Iron Historic District. Nearly forty years later, in 2010, the New York City Landmarks Preservation Commission designated new boundaries, adding a few extra streets to the east and west of the original borders. They called it the SoHo Cast-Iron Historic District Extension.

The purpose of this book is to take you on a very casual stroll around SoHo, visiting locations that evoke New York's colorful history. We'll go up and down the main streets, through the center of the neighborhood but also along its fringes. And although we will spend much of our time in the designated rectangle that is the most familiar part of SoHo, we might as well take advantage of the extended boundaries (more buildings to see, more stories to tell). The NYC Landmarks Preservation Commission includes twenty-six blocks and about five hundred buildings in the SoHo Cast-Iron Historic District, but we are going to wander just a bit beyond these boundaries and take a peek at a couple of locations that are just a little beyond the traditional SoHo borders. And if, from time to time, we find ourselves straying somewhat outside the neighborhood, we beg your indulgence (and invite you to join us).

During our tour of SoHo, we will tell you some stories that may surprise you, some forgotten tales of the city and some spicy ones as well. We may even include a ghost or two. And because SoHo is one of the most architecturally rich districts of New York City, we will visit a number of buildings that have histories and even personalities of their own, buildings that barely escaped destruction to make way for the infamous Lower Manhattan Expressway (the defeat of which is a major feather in the cap of the Landmarks Preservation Commission).

INTRODUCTION

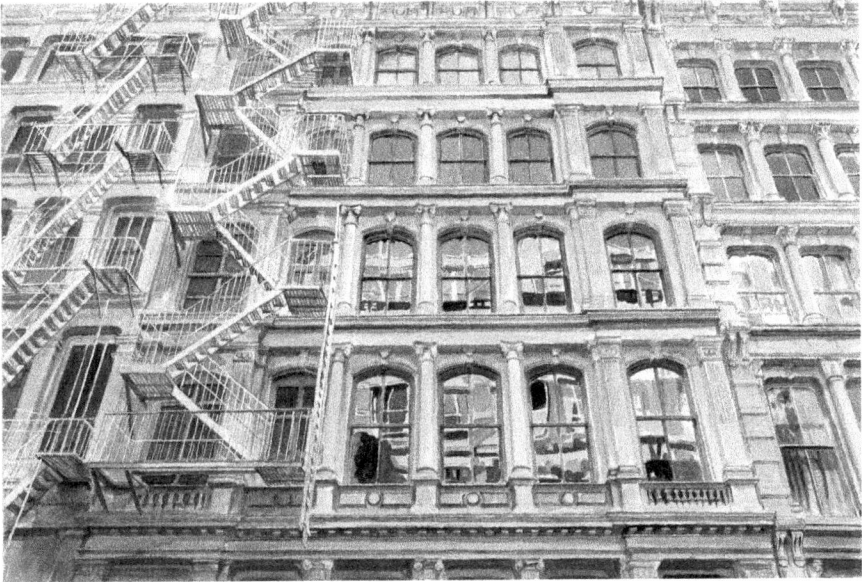

Cast-iron warehouses on Broome Street. *Watercolor by Leendert van der Pool.*

We invite you to sit back and enjoy this tour from the comfort of your armchair, or pick up this book and walk with us through these historic streets.

I

LOCAL HISTORY, PART I

Having established that the name "SoHo" is a mere sixty years old, the question arises: what was SoHo before it was SoHo?

The history of what we now call SoHo goes back to the settlement of Manhattan by the Dutch in the early seventeenth century and, prior to that, to the Native Americans who lived on Manhattan Island from time immemorial. Like much of Manhattan, the SoHo area was part of the hunting and fishing grounds of the Lenape Indians, who migrated seasonally from one part of the island to another. In fact, the trail that these Native Americans established from the top of Manhattan to the bottom (where Bowling Green is now located) would one day become Broadway.

Fortunately for the Dutch—and less so for the Native Americans—Peter Minuit struck a deal with the Lenape Indians, purchasing the island of Manhattan for sixty guilders in goods. This was in 1626, when Peter Minuit was the director of the Dutch West India Company (the VOC: Verenigde Oostindische Compagnie), and sixty guilders was worth somewhat more than it is today (today it's worth about twenty-five euros—think about that!). The Dutch West India Company undoubtedly knew that it was getting value for its money.

The majority of the early Dutch settlers lived considerably south of what we now define as SoHo's southern boundary, but the SoHo area was nevertheless inhabited. Some of the land was farmed by wealthy burghers, many of whom used their "country estates" to escape from the epidemics that regularly plagued the crowded New Amsterdam colony.

The SoHo area was, moreover, the location of the first free African American settlement on Manhattan Island, the so-called Free Negro Lots. These were farms that were offered to African slaves who were granted conditional freedom in 1644 by the Dutch West India Company. They were generally given title to the land they had already been farming. This region, a hilly area just north of the Lower Manhattan Dutch settlement, was seen as a buffer zone, serving as a first line of defense for the New Amsterdam inhabitants, protecting them from Indian attacks. But whether the land was freely granted or came with this unspoken condition—i.e., to serve as an "early warning system"—the former slaves were landowners, enjoying many of the same privileges as the Dutch settlers. In addition to the newly freed slaves, there were other African settlers farming the Free Negro Lots who had never been enslaved.

Incidentally, the first African slaves arrived in New Amsterdam as early as 1625, and many of them received partial freedom from the VOC twenty years later. Their status changed once again in 1665, when the British took control and New Amsterdam became New York. Within two years, the free African Americans were denied the privileges granted by the Dutch, including the right to own property. Many of the Free Negro Lots were deeded to white landowners, and having lost their land, the majority of the free Africans left Manhattan for Brooklyn and New Jersey.

New York's history in this regard was nothing to be proud of. The British established the first slave market in the colony (on Wall Street at the East River) in 1709. According to the United States National Park Service, in the early years of the eighteenth century, more than 40 percent of New York households had slaves. New York had the second-largest number of slaves in the American colonies, second only to South Carolina, and was, moreover, one of the last northern states to abolish slavery; this did not happen until 1827.

Although some African Americans remained in the SoHo area—mainly as slaves working for white property owners—the land was gradually acquired by one Augustine Herrman (1605–1686), a fur trader, slave trader and tobacco exporter who came to the Dutch colony from Prague via Amsterdam and amassed a huge fortune. He purchased land for himself and his brother-in-law, Nicholas Bayard, who inherited all of the SoHo landholdings at Herrman's death.

(Herrman spent the last twenty-five years of his life in Maryland, where he had been sent by Peter Stuyvesant to negotiate the boundaries between the Maryland Territory and the Dutch colony. He spent ten of those years drawing up a map of the Maryland Territory, for which Lord Baltimore rewarded him with more than thirteen thousand acres of land and the title "Lord of the Manor." (This has nothing to do with SoHo, but it's an interesting story.)

The vast Bayard Farm was to play a part in the history of Alexander Hamilton, who died at the Bayard farmhouse after his fateful (and unsuccessful) duel with Aaron Burr in 1804.

In addition to being Augustine Herrman's brother-in-law, Nicholas Bayard (1644–1707) was the nephew of Peter Stuyvesant. As mayor of New Amsterdam, Bayard was instrumental in the implementation of the Dongan Charter (1686), which not only guaranteed rights to colonial citizens but also laid the groundwork for the establishment of New York City's first public parks. Bayard, one of the biggest landowners in the colony, became embroiled in a popular rebellion in 1689—unfortunately on the wrong side. Accused of treason and piracy in collaboration with Captain Kidd, Bayard was stripped of his property and sentenced to be hanged, drawn and quartered. He wisely fled the city. To his good fortune, the ruling was overturned, and Bayard's property was once again secured. The Bayard landholdings remained in the family until after the Revolutionary War, at which time economic exigencies forced the family (Nicholas Bayard III, in fact) to sell the land. It was thereupon divided into lots, and in the early nineteenth century, the beginnings of SoHo's street plan emerged.

The SoHo landscape back in the seventeenth and eighteenth centuries was quite different from the relatively flat land on which these new streets were surveyed. For one thing, the land was hilly, with such recognizable landmarks as Bayard's Hill, Cripplebush Swamp (great name!), Smith's Hill and the stream that would become Canal Street (more about that in Chapter 3). Many of the original street names were later changed, but the grid today is very similar to the one laid out after Bayard sold his farms.

A curious feature of the SoHo street plan, by the way—and one that hasn't been altered—is that the longer streets run north–south and the shorter ones run east–west. Oddly, the wider streets in SoHo are east–west streets, and the narrower ones run north–south (are you following?). New York City above Fourteenth Street has an entirely different pattern, with north–south streets being both longer and wider than east–west streets.

Development came fast to these newly designated lots, and Broadway quickly became the main thoroughfare. In fact, even before the arrival of the British, Broadway was a busy residential and commercial street—called "De Heere Straat" by the Dutch and renamed "Broad Way" by the British.

Broadway, looking south from Houston Street, 1868. *Courtesy of Dover Publications, Inc.*

During the first half of the eighteenth century, New York City continued to expand northward. By 1775, Broadway had been extended north of Canal Street as far as Astor Place (a few blocks above our SoHo boundary). In 1809, the street was paved, and sidewalks were laid. Row houses were built; brick one-family, two- and three-story Federal-style buildings housed the middle and more privileged classes, as well as artisans. These houses and a few free-standing buildings shared the streets with small shops and stables. And nearby, the wealthy built mansions. John Jacob Astor lived in his palatial home on the corner of Broadway and Prince Street, where he died in 1848. We'll hear more about him in Chapter 8.

Local History, Part I

By the 1840s, the streets between Canal and Houston, from river to river (the East River to the Hudson), were fully developed, and the SoHo area was the most densely populated part of New York City. All this changed in the middle of the century. The cast-iron architectural revolution was approaching.

LOCAL HISTORY, PART II

The 1850s and 1860s brought great changes to SoHo. Within a few years, the quiet residential streets were transformed into a neighborhood of theaters, grand hotels and fashionable shops.

It all started on Broadway, where a growing number of retail shops started to appear, many having moved from below Canal Street, in order to serve the swelling population of the neighborhood. Small stores gave way to larger ones, and soon SoHo became Manhattan's premier shopping district. Department stores such as Lord & Taylor, Brooks Brothers and Tiffany's replaced the mansions on Broadway, and multi-story buildings were erected, attracting crowds of shoppers tempted by a vast array of consumer goods, everything they ever needed or wanted.

The same years saw the arrival of new and elegant hotels opening along Broadway, many of which achieved widespread fame. Music halls and theaters soon followed, and Broadway, from Canal Street to Houston Street, became New York's center of entertainment and spectacle. The new department stores and theaters were built of marble, brownstone and—as we shall soon see—cast iron.

And along with the hotels and theaters, there emerged a large and well-patronized red-light district, with brothels located in the streets near Broadway. Mercer, Greene and Crosby Streets were well known for their "ladies' boarding houses," as were West Broadway and Houston Street, where a variety of pleasures could be purchased. Many of the SoHo brothels offered specialties—French, German or Creole hostesses, for

Metropolitan Hotel interior, 1860. *Courtesy of Dover Publications, Inc.*

example—and guidebooks could be purchased enabling customers to find whatever they desired.

The streets to the east and west of Broadway also saw dramatic changes during these decades. Industrial and commercial enterprises replaced many of the Federal-style residences. In some cases, the original buildings were used for commercial purposes; elsewhere, new buildings were erected. Light industry, such as doll makers, furriers, paper box manufacturers and clothing factories, replaced the one-family homes. By 1870, the streets of SoHo had been transformed into a lively commercial and industrial area, and along Broadway, the entertainment district continued to thrive. Many families fled, once again moving farther north on Manhattan Island.

Underlying these socioeconomic changes was one of the most dramatic—and beautiful—architectural innovations of modern times: the invention of the cast-iron façade.

Cast iron itself had been around for centuries, but it wasn't until the mid-eighteenth century that it could be produced inexpensively enough to make it attractive to architects. Prior to then, it was used primarily for tools and machinery, cooking utensils, cannons and ammunition. For the material to be used effectively, the iron had to be refined: heated, melted and the impurities removed. It could then be poured into molds and formed into prefabricated parts. And in the nineteenth century, new, more efficient furnaces made this process easier, faster and cheaper. With the improvement of this previously slow and expensive process, cast iron began to be widely employed.

In the early years of the nineteenth century, cast iron was mainly used to make stair rails, balconies, door and window frames and other interior and exterior building parts, but by mid-century, local New York foundries had started producing columns both for internal support and for the outside of buildings. Because of the enormous tensile strength of cast iron, these columns could be manufactured taller and much more slender than the heavy stone supports previously used. Shops, factories and warehouses were constructed with large, open work spaces, and when used on the exterior, cast-iron window frames could be installed, capable of supporting unprecedentedly large glass windows, which allowed natural light and fresh air to flood the interiors. For the first time, retail stores were fashioned

Number 429 Broadway, at the corner of Howard Street.

The cover of a Badger catalogue, 1865. *Courtesy of Dover Publications, Inc.*

with vast show windows to display their merchandise, and factories and warehouses could be similarly well lit.

Typically, these mid-century cast-iron buildings were built to a height of four-to-six stories, the number of levels being limited because they had to be reached by stairs. New developments in elevator design, a few years later, would change that. (We'll hear about Mr. Otis and his safety elevator in a later chapter.)

The iron-casting process, moreover, allowed architects to design prefabricated building façades in a vast range of styles, with a great variety of ornamentation and decoration. Where masonry (stone) buildings often took many years to complete, a cast-iron façade could be molded in a foundry, shipped in parts and assembled—bolted together—at the location where it was to be installed, all in a matter of a few months. And the molds could be used repeatedly so that architectural elements could be reproduced in multiples and shipped anywhere in the country for installation. The process, in brief, saved time and money and allowed architects enhanced freedom of design.

The economic and aesthetic advantages of cast iron led to vast changes on the streets of SoHo. New buildings were constructed of iron, and existing ones had cast-iron façades superimposed over brick and masonry structures. Huge, light-filled retail palaces were erected, and the design of hotels and theaters underwent a revolution as well.

An interesting aspect of cast-iron architecture was that the façades were often painted to resemble stone. Decorative features of the buildings, such as fluted columns and Corinthian capitals, imitated designs previously carved in Italianate, Classical, Renaissance Revival or French Beaux-Arts façades, and to maintain the illusion, the architects or building owners had the façades painted white or off-white so they would appear to be made of stone.

SoHo has the largest concentration of full or partial cast-iron façades in the world. During our tour of the neighborhood, we will visit a number of these buildings, many of which have achieved landmark status. The years have taken their toll, and many are no longer in very good condition; even more distressingly, the street-level façades have generally been replaced by contemporary retail storefronts, to the detriment of the streetscape. But if we raise our eyes, we'll see an astonishing array of extraordinary buildings. As we walk along, we'll also hear about some of the cast-iron innovators who made this revolution happen. We will make the acquaintance of, among others, architect and foundry owner Daniel Badger, as well as Ernest Flagg, who built the Singer Tower, which was, for one year, the tallest building in

Helmbold's Drugstore interior, Broadway, 1875. *Courtesy of Dover Publications, Inc.*

the world. (In fact, the Singer Tower was not a cast-iron building, although Flagg used cast iron in many of his other constructions.)

The peak of the cast-iron age was during the second half of the nineteenth century. In fact, the majority of SoHo's iron-framed department stores, factories, warehouses and hotels were built—or their façades were installed—between 1850 and 1880. Not all of these buildings are still standing, but thanks to the New York City Landmarks Preservation Commission, those that remain are safe from the wrecker's ball.

By the end of the nineteenth century, steel began to replace iron, which couldn't compete with the cost or strength of this new building material. But there were other reasons why cast iron fell out of favor. Once touted

Number 462 Broadway, with its cast-iron façade.

as fireproof, it began to be apparent that this wasn't true. In the event of a fire, cast-iron support beams turned brittle, often cracking under high heat, which resulted in more than one disastrous building collapse. Furthermore, many of the cast-iron façades were built over wooden structures, which of course were far from fireproof. A number of deadly fires eventually convinced builders that cast iron was not effectively fireproof.

During the heyday of the cast-iron era, SoHo was home to a slew of large and prosperous manufacturing corporations, as well as the main offices of a number of worldwide businesses. Lorillard's Snuff Manufactory, for example, occupied an entire city block from Broome Street to Spring Street, Wooster Street to West Broadway. Other buildings housed dry goods and textile companies, doing many millions of dollars worth of business per annum. A New York & New Haven Railroad freight depot on Canal Street at the southeastern corner of SoHo, located between Elm Street (today's Lafayette Street) and Centre Street, enhanced the commercial and industrial desirability of the area, as did the proximity of the Hudson River docks. Access to the area was further facilitated by the Metropolitan Elevated Railway, which opened in 1878 and part of which ran along West Broadway.

But this prosperity was short-lived. Within a few years, there was a mass exodus from SoHo, both commercially and residentially, and the neighborhood began a steep decline.

Even before the end of the century—in fact, starting in the 1870s—Broadway's elegant department stores began to move north, abandoning their cast-iron palaces and relocating in what became known as "the Ladies' Mile," an area that included Broadway and Fifth and Sixth Avenues between Tenth and Twenty-fourth Streets. The entertainment district, too, had moved uptown, replaced by factories, warehouses and retail businesses. But in the closing years of the nineteenth century, most of these larger businesses deserted the SoHo neighborhood as well. Small factories and marginal warehouses occupied the once-bustling commercial streets. The population of SoHo shrank to a new low, and many buildings were allowed to decay and even lie empty.

Not a lot changed, certainly not for the better, during the first half of the twentieth century. Along the fringes of SoHo, tenements were constructed, built to house many families per floor, without the luxury of indoor plumbing. A number of these buildings still exist on Crosby Street, though they are no longer classifiable as slum dwellings (quite the contrary!). Some of the deserted buildings were torn down during the Depression, as businesses continued to abandon the area for the less-expensive suburbs or simply close their doors forever. According to the Landmarks Commission, by the 1950s, SoHo reported a 15 percent vacancy rate, and lofts could be rented for fifty cents per square foot or less. Even in 1950, that was a pretty good price—though the buildings were often badly deteriorated and fell far short of city safety standards.

The fortunes of SoHo may have reached their lowest point when fire commissioner Edward Cavanagh Jr. (who served between 1954 and 1962) designated SoHo and Tribeca (or what was later known as Tribeca) as "Hell's Hundred Acres." This dire appellation was given to a large area comprising the streets between Broadway and the Hudson River, from Chambers Street in Lower Manhattan to Houston Street, an area plagued by numerous deadly fires in the old industrial buildings.

(Having said that, we should confess that these boundaries vary from one contemporary report to another. According to the *New York Times*, for example, in an article published in 1966, "Hell's Hundred Acres" extended between Grand Street and Houston Street, Lafayette Street and the river. Other sources cite Eighth Street, rather than Houston, as the northern boundary and Reade, rather than Chambers Street, as the southern.

A Shaft sign on Mercer Street. *Courtesy of Leendert van der Pool.*

(Whichever source you choose, however, pretty much all of SoHo was included in this calamitous area.)

Long neglected, too many of these buildings were in violation of New York City fire codes, with fragile wooden floors and stairways (weakened by heavy loads), narrow passageways and doors that were nailed shut. Electrical wiring was worn out or inadequate, adding immeasurably to the risk of fires. Often used as warehouses, overloaded with flammable goods and "dead storage"—i.e., bulky waste paper and rags—many of the industrial buildings lacked sprinkler systems, and fire spread rapidly from floor to floor and building to building. Furthermore, many factories had windows in their elevator shafts, so firemen trying to gain access through a window were in danger of falling down the elevator shaft, often to their deaths. A law was eventually passed requiring buildings to have large signs reading, "Shaft" installed on the outside, where these windows were located. (Have you ever wondered what those Shaft signs are for? Now you know.) But before the signs were installed and before the city began to enforce its fire regulations more vigorously, many firemen perished, and Hell's Hundred Acres had earned its name.

The large number of fatal fires in the early to mid-1960s finally resulted in an intensified fire prevention campaign, but not before lives were lost and many of the city's nineteenth-century buildings were destroyed. In addition to fires, the floors of many of the older industrial buildings in SoHo were in danger of collapsing because of excessive weight. According to a *New York Times* article in February 1966, the New York Buildings Department reported "violations in 356 of the 911 buildings inspected, 123 floors that appeared to be overloaded and 59 structural defects."

By the mid-1960s, much of the light industry that had been in place in SoHo for half a century (and more) had moved out of the city. SoHo seemed to be in the last stages of decrepitude when a few enterprising young artists came along and turned it all around. A new chapter in the history of SoHo was about to be written: the Age of the Artists!

How did SoHo become a mecca for contemporary art? How does any neighborhood evolve socially, economically or ethnically? That's not an easy question to answer, but what probably happened in SoHo is typical: a few impoverished artists discovered that big, open loft spaces with high ceilings and lots of natural light could be had for a pittance. Where else in Manhattan could a struggling artist have this luxury of space—to say nothing of huge windows and very few neighbors? One artist followed another, and soon the formerly abandoned industrial lofts saw new life as artists' studios; SoHo began to reinvent itself once again. (And let's not forget, this is when SoHo was first called "SoHo.")

We'll learn more about SoHo's rise—and demise—as the vortex of New York's contemporary art scene, a vibrant district of artists, galleries and (often illegal) converted living/working spaces, as we stroll through this ever-evolving neighborhood.

SoHo's preeminence as New York's contemporary art center lasted only a few decades. At its peak, in the late 1970s, about five thousand artists were living in SoHo, and many of the world's most fashionable (and expensive) galleries had their addresses along West Broadway. What happened toward the end of the twentieth century is a common tale of urban development, gentrification and corporate greed. As SoHo achieved international renown, rents went up, up, up, and before long, many artists could no longer afford to live there. And who moved in? The rich and the famous, movie stars and media moguls, young and wealthy professionals, supermodels and superstar athletes (and a few corporate lawyers as well). The galleries, of which there were over 150 at the end of the twentieth century, moved north and west to Chelsea, and once again, expensive retail stores moved in, just as they had done a century and a half earlier. To paraphrase Yogi Berra, "It was déjà vu all over again."

SoHo today is a neighborhood of exclusive shops and restaurants, newly renovated or newly built luxury condos and a number of boutique hotels. But there are still 150 carefully preserved cast-iron buildings, as well as architectural gems of stone and brick, all under the watchful eye of New York's Landmarks Commission. The streets are crowded on weekend afternoons and evenings with tourists visiting the shops, restaurants and clubs, but if you go out early in the morning and wander these historic streets, you can easily appreciate the magnificence of the architecture and the time-worn stones that still pave the streets.

And that's just what we are going to do—take a walk, look around and hear (or read) some New York stories.

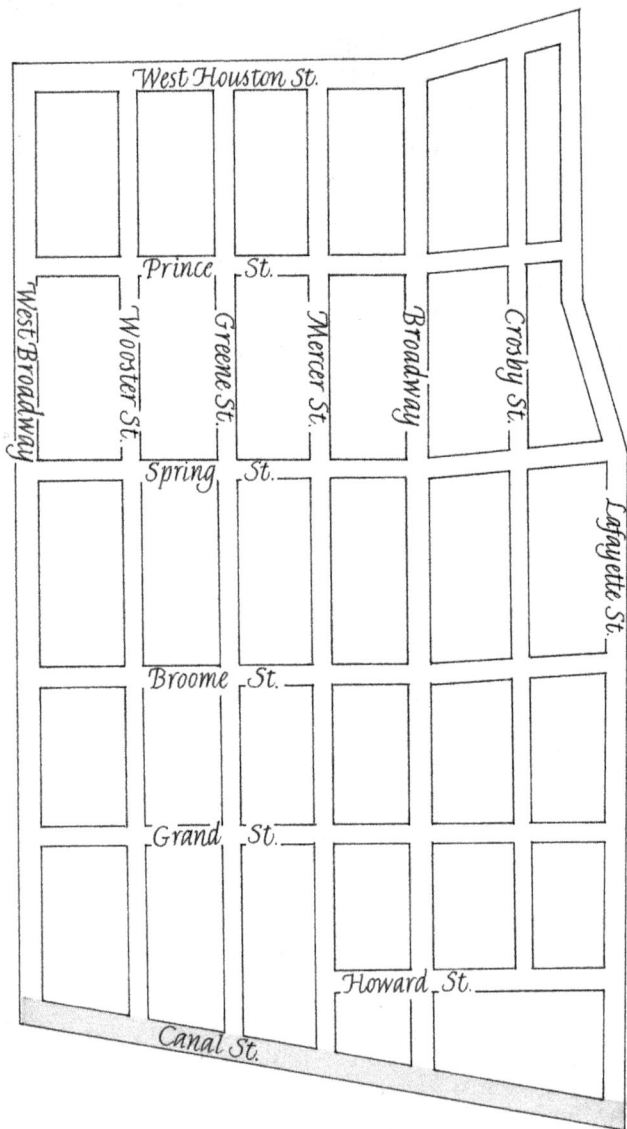

CANAL STREET

The Collect Pond, Bogardus and Bruce,
Blackwell's Island and Samuel F.B. Morse

Standing on the corner of Canal and Lafayette Street—at the southeast corner of the SoHo Cast-Iron Historic District—it is almost impossible to picture the smelly stream of polluted greenish sludge that once followed the route of today's noisy, colorful, traffic-clogged thoroughfare.

In the eighteenth century, Canal Street was not yet in existence. Still north of the city line, a stream ran along here that served as an outlet for the now-forgotten Collect Pond, ending in marshlands on the west side of Manhattan Island. What was the Collect Pond? Also known as "Fresh Water Pond," this was a seventy-acre, sixty-foot-deep pool of water fed by an underground spring. The Collect Pond was located a block or so below today's Canal Street and extended south to the (current) City Hall neighborhood. At one time used for ice-skating in the winter and picnics during the summer months, it was originally Manhattan's source of drinking water. But by the end of the eighteenth century, the Collect had become no better than a sewer, serving as a dumping ground for all kinds of waste: dead animals, human filth and detritus from tanneries, breweries, furnaces and other local industry, many of which were located right on the perimeter of the Collect.

(The derivation of the name "Collect" seems to be open to a variety of options. According to one source, it's from the Dutch *Kalck Hoek*, meaning "shell hook," so called because of the oyster shells that the indigenous Indians left behind. Other sources say it's from the word *Kolch*, also a Dutch word, meaning "pond," and yet another—this one a modern Dutch source—suggests that the

Traffic on Canal Street. *Courtesy of Leendert van der Pool.*

word comes from *Kolk*, which is a basin located outside a lock used for stabilizing ships. (What an inexact science is history!)

But whatever derivation you prefer, by the closing years of the eighteenth century, the Collect Pond was recognized as a blot on the landscape and was, moreover, a breeding ground for cholera, yellow fever and other deadly diseases. The city had to take action, and following a yellow fever epidemic in 1798 that left nearly 2,100 dead (about 7 percent of the population of Manhattan), the Common Council (city government) made plans to fill in the pond and drain the surrounding swamplands. In order to do this, a forty-foot-wide drainage canal was dug along what would become Canal Street, wider and deeper than the existing stream, with the purpose of emptying the water from the Collect Pond into the Hudson River. Within ten years, the Collect Pond was gone, but the new canal had become, in its turn, no better than a sewer. Shortly thereafter, it too was covered, and by 1817, Canal Street was paved.

This might have been the end of the story of the Collect Pond had the landfill been done correctly. A new neighborhood, known (ironically, given its history) as Paradise Square, was built over the Collect Pond landfill, but because the foundations of the houses were on swampland, the buildings began to sink almost immediately. To make matters worse, the water trapped underground made the area smell horrible, and the more affluent residents of the district fled as quickly as possible.

Within a few years, Paradise Square became known as Five Points, named for the five corners at the intersection of three of its streets, and the neighborhood lay just adjacent to the southeastern border of today's SoHo. An area of poverty, overpopulation, desperation and crime, Five Points was home to some of the notorious street gangs that ruled parts of Lower Manhattan during the nineteenth century and was, not surprisingly, one of the hardest hit during the frequent epidemics that plagued the city. (A few recent movies have glamorized Five Points and its colorful inhabitants, but it was a very bad place indeed, which has, fortunately, disappeared off the map.)

On the other (north) side of Canal Street, the situation during the nineteenth century was quite different. Once the canal was paved over, the middle class started moving in, followed by shops and businesses. For about fifty years, the neighborhood north of Canal Street flourished as a residential and artisan district, worlds away from the squalor of Five Points.

Well, we seem to have diverged from our path without getting very far...

It's time to take a look at some of the buildings on Canal Street. Right here, at our starting point, on the west side of Lafayette Street, is one of New York's great buildings and one of the first with a cast-iron façade. Located at 254 Canal Street, it was built in 1857, possibly by James Bogardus. Why "possibly"? And who was James Bogardus?

The answer to the first question is at best vague. Records are sketchy about the origins of 254 Canal, no doubt because New York City did not require building permits until 1866. But experts seem to agree that it has many features resembling other buildings designed by Bogardus.

James Bogardus (1800–1874) was a native New Yorker. Without much formal education, he quickly earned a reputation as an inventor, credited with, among other things, a postage stamp engraving machine, a cotton-spinning machine and deep-sea drilling equipment. But he is best known as the innovative architect who designed and built the first cast-iron buildings in New York.

A successful entrepreneur, Bogardus called himself an "Architect in Iron" and, in 1849, built his own all-iron factory on Duane Street in New York in which he constructed prefabricated building parts—columns, beams, walls, frames and façades. In 1850, he took out a patent for the construction of "the frame, roof and floor of iron buildings"; in other words, for using cast iron not just for decoration and architectural detail but also as a structural material. Bogardus is recognized as a pioneer, the instigator of the cast-iron

Number 254 Canal Street.

revolution that swept America in the second half of the nineteenth century and led to the development of steel-framed buildings.

Now here's a strange tale. Another of Bogardus's cast-iron buildings, a five-story department store that once stood at Washington Street and Murray Street in Lower Manhattan, was removed in the early 1970s to make way for a new building. The component parts were carefully disassembled and stored in order to be reassembled at another location. Somehow these cast-iron building parts were stolen from their storage location and melted. This, says the *AIA Guide to New York City*, was "the first building ever physically stolen." (One might well wonder *how* one steals a building, as well as who stole it.)

Number 254 Canal Street was one of the first large commercial buildings in SoHo. It is not only an impressive building but was also built for an important figure in the history of printing: George Bruce (1781–1866). In fact, it's sometimes known as the George Bruce Building. Born in Scotland, Bruce arrived in 1795 in Philadelphia, where he learned the printing trade. He and his brother David moved to New York a few years later and soon made their reputations—and fortunes—as innovators in printing technology, including the invention of a type-casting machine and the introduction (in the United States) of stereotyping, a process that made book and newspaper printing cheaper and faster.

George Bruce, renowned in his day as a printer and typographer, ran the largest type foundry in America. He also became very rich. In a 1910 article published fifty years after his death (entitled "Bruce Estate Auction Sale...Biggest Realty Event in Many Years"), the *New York Times* wrote that he "made wise investments in real estate." These included 254 Canal Street and other properties scattered throughout SoHo, as well as numerous locations up and down Manhattan Island, real estate worth upward of $3 million.

Did George Bruce ever actually set up shop in the George Bruce Building in SoHo? The records once again are a bit confusing. An 1884 *History of New York Publishing* says that he spent his working life—from 1818 until his death forty-eight years later—at his foundry on Chambers Street. Other sources seem to indicate that 254 Canal Street was custom built for George Bruce's printing business but was occupied by a textile merchant during the 1860s, followed by a tobacco dealer. But the building is still known as the George Bruce Building, and it is still attributed (with a few reservations) to James Bogardus. Perhaps someone will make a definitive decision about this, but meanwhile, let's see what else happened on Canal Street.

Across the street from the George Bruce Building, the first St. Vincent de Paul Catholic Church once stood. It was the parish church of New York's French-

Early morning on Canal Street (before the crowds arrive).

speaking population from 1841 until 1857. In the early years of the nineteenth century, there was a large French community in Manhattan, but it wasn't until the opening of St. Vincent de Paul that they had their own church. In fact, for about fifteen years before the church was established, the bishop of New York had been a Frenchman, John Dubois. (By the 1840s, however, the Irish Catholic community in the city outnumbered the French, and upon Bishop Dubois' death in 1842, an Irish bishop from Philadelphia, John Joseph Hughes, became bishop of New York. The diocese of New York, by the way, was established in 1808. Dubois was the third bishop. His successor, the aforementioned John Hughes, was the fourth bishop, but when the diocese was raised to an archdiocese in 1850, Hughes became the first archbishop of New York. All the bishops who preceded Dubois and all the archbishops who followed Hughes have been Irish.) We'll hear more about Bishop Hughes in Chapter 9.

St. Vincent de Paul, also known as the French Church, was the first Catholic church in New York to offer Masses in French, but the church itself survived for only a few years. By the 1850s, a large part of the French population had moved uptown, and in 1857, the cornerstone of the new St. Vincent de Paul on Twenty-third Street was laid. It opened in 1868 and still offers masses in French. (Interesting fact: in 1952, Edith Piaf was married to French singer and actor Jacques Pills at St. Vincent de Paul; the marriage lasted three years. Piaf's matron of honor was Marlene Dietrich.)

A parochial school, St. Vincent de Paul Academy, was also built on Canal Street and was run by the Christian Brothers, four of whom came over from France in 1848 to establish the school. Like the original church building, the school has also disappeared, although the Christian Brothers have been instrumental in the spread of Catholic education worldwide. (The founders of the school on Canal Street were French Christian Brothers, known as the "De La Salle Christian Brothers"; there is a separate order from Ireland. Both orders have been influential in the history of Catholic education.)

Let's pause for a moment on the northwest corner of Broadway and Canal Street, where shoppers and tourists fill today's crowded streets. In the early years of the nineteenth century, this was the location of the cast-iron foundry of Joseph Blackwell. Blackwell's name is familiar to us for reasons other than his contributions to the cast-iron historic district. The name Blackwell, not so very long ago, evoked the fearsome history of Blackwell's Island.

Back in the early years of New York City, large parcels of land were owned by individual landowners (remember Nicholas Bayard? Peter Stuyvesant?). One of these was Robert Blackwell (1643–1717), who arrived in New Amsterdam in the late seventeenth century and acquired what are now Astoria, Long Island City, Green Point and Williamsburg (yes, it's hard to imagine). He also acquired a wife, Mary Manningham, whose stepfather, John Manning, owned Manning Island in the East River. At the time of their marriage, Mary Manningham and Robert Blackwell settled on Manning Island, which thereafter became known as Blackwell's Island.

(This wasn't the first time the name of the island was changed. Going back a bit further in history, the Dutch governor of New Amsterdam, Wouter van Twiller, purchased the island from Native Americans. In the seventeenth century, it was known as Hog Island, in honor of the pigs the Dutch raised there. When Manning bought it in 1668, he renamed the island after himself. Blackwell did the same thing.)

But why is Blackwell's Island notorious? In 1828, the New York City Common Council bought the island from James Blackwell, a descendant of Robert, for the purpose of building a penitentiary, as well as facilities for the poor, the mad and the sick. In 1832, the first buildings of the penitentiary were erected, followed, by mid-century, by additional prison buildings, an almshouse, a hospital for incurables, a workhouse (which served as a prison for minor offenders) and the New York City Lunatic Asylum. Opened in 1839, this was the first publicly funded mental institution in the country.

Not surprisingly, Blackwell's Island was soon overcrowded, with seven thousand of the city's unwanted occupying the 120-acre island. And conditions in the insane asylum—which was guarded and staffed by convicts from the penitentiary—were particularly dire.

Which brings us to the story of Nellie Bly, a young journalist who exposed the scandal of the Blackwell's Island Asylum for the Insane in a series of articles for the *New York World* in 1887. Bly, whose real name was Elizabeth Cochrane, was twenty-three at the time; she was admitted as an inmate to the asylum by pretending to be mad and stayed for ten days, until her newspaper managed to get her discharged. Considered to be the first female "stunt reporter"—i.e., a reporter who goes underground to get her story—Bly was paid twenty-five dollars by Joseph Pulitzer for her story about Blackwell's Island. The articles she wrote for the *World* exposed the appalling conditions at the asylum, which she termed a "human rat trap." These were later published in a book entitled *Ten Days in a Mad-House*, and within a few years, the asylum was shut down.

The penitentiary lasted nearly forty years longer. It, too, was plagued by inhumane conditions and was permanently closed in 1934, after decades of scandals. Inmates were transferred to Riker's Island, and not surprisingly, the name of the island was changed. As a matter of fact, Blackwell's Island had already been renamed Welfare Island in 1921, a move by the city to

Blackwell's Island prison, 1853. *Watercolor by Leendert van der Pool.*

improve its image. In 1973, it became Roosevelt Island, which today is a thriving residential community connected to Manhattan by a tramway.

And now let's return to the streets of SoHo.

The story of Canal Street, like much of New York City, contains a lot of "used to's." One example is New York's only Bulgarian bar, which used to be on the corner of Canal and Broadway; it has since relocated to the Lower East Side.

About 150 years before the Bulgarian bar had its day, a prominent resident of Canal Street was Samuel F.B. Morse (1791–1872), whom we remember best as the inventor of the Morse code. The telegraph, first built in 1774, was a complicated system, involving twenty-six wires (one for each letter of the alphabet). To reduce its complexity, Morse and his partner, Alfred Vail, developed a single-wire system that worked with a dot-and-dash code. They demonstrated their invention in 1844, sending the first inter-city message from Washington to Baltimore: "What hath God wrought?"

It was two decades prior to this historic moment that Morse, then an artist specializing in portraiture, rented a house on Canal Street. According to his journals (which were published in 1914), his rent was $400 per year. He wrote, "I do not think its being so far 'uptown' will, on the whole, be any disadvantage to me." During his years on Canal Street, Morse was hired as a professor of painting and sculpture at New York University, where he remained between 1832 and 1841. One of his paintings was entitled *Allegorical Landscape of New York University.* (Morse also painted a full-sized portrait of Lafayette, which still hangs in city hall.) Samuel F.B. Morse was also the founder and first president of the National Academy of Design and ran for mayor of New York twice, both times unsuccessfully. And this was all before he became interested in telegraphy.

And what about today's Canal Street? What do we see when we look left and right along this broad avenue? Well, for one thing, it's hard to see very far; at almost anytime of day, Canal Street is thronged with crowds and jammed with traffic. The stretch between Lafayette Street and West Broadway is one of the busiest streets in Manhattan and has become one of New York's liveliest shopping streets. Where else can you buy a Rolex for ten dollars? Designer knock-offs (or fakes) abound, as do electronics, jewelry, handbags, clothing and New York souvenirs, much of it available from open-front stores and street stalls.

Long recognized as the dividing line between Little Italy and Chinatown, the boundaries have become a little more indefinite, as the local Chinese population increases and the Italian one decreases. But since neither Chinatown nor Little Italy is, strictly speaking, part of our tour of SoHo, we're going to move along to the eastern boundary of SoHo and see what Crosby Street has to offer.

Open-air shopping on Canal Street. *Courtesy of Leendert van der Pool.*

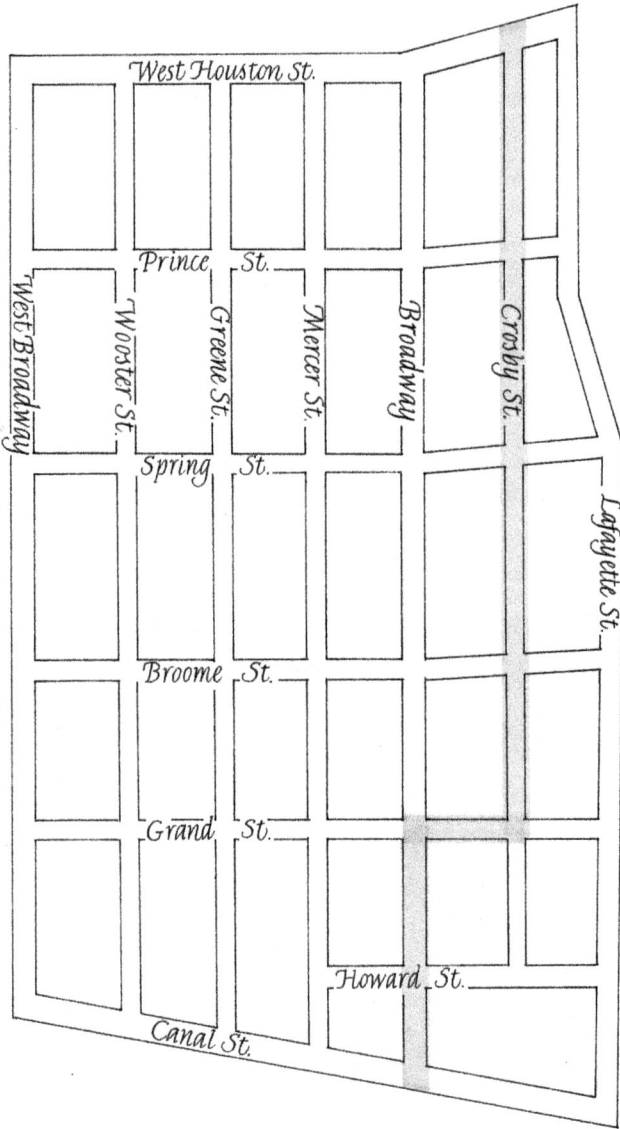

West Houston St.

Prince St.

West Broadway

Wooster St.

Greene St.

Mercer St.

Broadway

Crosby St.

Lafayette St.

Spring St.

Broome St.

Grand St.

Howard St.

Canal St.

4

ALONG CROSBY STREET AND
BACK TO GRAND STREET

An Opium Den, the First Jewish Congregation,
Department Stores, Spiritualists and Séances

Having left Canal Street, the southern border of SoHo, we now head north along Crosby Street. Ever since the New York City Landmarks Preservation Commission extended the eastern boundary of the historic district, Crosby Street has been well inside SoHo rather than at the extreme edge. (In fact, at one time, only the west side of Crosby Street was considered part of SoHo; now, the east side of the street is included as well, plus another block or two beyond.)

Crosby Street, however, feels a bit like a quiet back road, with the boom and bustle of Broadway attracting the attention of most SoHo visitors.

In the old days, during the last decades of the nineteenth century, Crosby Street was very much in the shadow of Broadway. A street of small factories and tenement houses, Crosby Street was not quite at the dismal level of the Five Points neighborhood (immediately to the southeast), but it was hardly a desirable address. An opium den, located at 53 Crosby near Broome Street, was the subject of a detailed article in the *New York Times* on July 2, 1885, reporting that a twenty-four-year-old cab driver died of what was probably an overdose. Said the *Times*, "[The autopsy showed that the victim] was a young man not unaccustomed to dissipation, and that organic troubles, suddenly aggravated by alcohol and the fumes of opium, had killed him." The party that night was a wild one. "Tenants of the neighboring houses, accustomed as they are to queer sights, were shocked to see people running in and out of No. 53 in a state of semi-nakedness—one or two of them wholly nude—and comporting themselves in a manner altogether disgraceful."

Crosby Street, looking south from Prince Street.

By the time the police arrived, the revelers had fled, and the opium "joint" (as the newspaper called it) had been abandoned. The proprietor tiptoed back the following night but was grabbed by the police and taken to the police station, accompanied by a large crowd of indignant neighbors.

Neither the opium den nor the building that housed it remains, but right across the street, at 56–62 Crosby Street, Shearith Israel Synagogue, the first Jewish congregation in North America, had its home from 1833 until 1860. (Apparently, the opium den arrived after the synagogue left.)

Not only was Shearith Israel the first Jewish congregation, but it also remained the *only* one in New York City for 175 years. It was founded in 1654 by twenty-three Spanish and Portuguese Jews who arrived unexpectedly in New Amsterdam from Brazil. Their story is interesting. Persecuted by the Spanish Inquisition, a number of Sephardic Jews fled Spain and Portugal and lived for a time in Holland. Employed by the Dutch West India Company, they were sent to Brazil, where they remained briefly before they found themselves, once again, victims of religious persecution and attempted to return to Europe.

En route back to Holland, a ship carrying the twenty-three Jewish settlers was attacked by pirates, who set them ashore on an island in the Caribbean. A passing ship, the *Saint Catherine*, picked them up and brought them to the Dutch colony, where they were reluctantly received by Governor Peter Stuyvesant. An anti-Semite, Stuyvesant allowed the Jewish settlers to remain only when pressured to do so by the Dutch West India Company (which was not only their employer but his as well). Once they were granted the right to live in New Amsterdam, they established their congregation, which became known as the Spanish and Portuguese Synagogue.

It wasn't until seventy-five years later, well after the British replaced the Dutch and New Amsterdam became New York, that the Shearith Israel Congregation had its own synagogue, which was built on Mill Street (now South William Street in the Wall Street area of Manhattan) in 1730. The building on Crosby Street was the congregation's third synagogue; Shearith Israel remained there for twenty-seven years.

In 1845, during the period that Shearith Israel was located on Crosby Street, Jacques Judah Lyons, the *chazan* (prayer leader), addressed his congregation, urging its members to donate money to help the starving population of Ireland during the potato famine. Lyons, who was the uncle of Emma Lazarus, collected $200 in a single evening, a large sum of money in those days. Additional contributions from Shearith Israel and another congregation, Shaaray Tefila (founded in 1845 on Wooster Street, a few blocks west of Crosby Street, and located today on the Upper East Side) brought the sum up to $1,000.

When Mary McAleese, president of Ireland, came to New York in 2010, she visited Shearith Israel to thank the congregation for its generosity, 163 years after they sent aid to Ireland.

In 1855, Jacques Judah Lyons helped found the Jews' Hospital, a forty-five-bed charity hospital for impoverished Jews that soon became known as Mount Sinai Hospital; this once small hospital is now Mount Sinai Medical Center and has well over one thousand beds, 2,200 attending physicians and 1,800 nurses.

Shearith Israel and its rabbis played a significant part in the development of many American Jewish institutions, including the founding of the American Jewish Theological Seminary in 1886. The congregation had two other addresses after Crosby Street and is now located on West Seventieth Street, where a plaque was installed in 1954, commemorating three hundred

Housing Works Bookstore, Crosby Street.

years "of faith and freedom." The synagogue on the Upper West Side is a New York City Landmark.

Crosby Street, by the way, was named after William Bedlow Crosby. Crosby (1786–1865) was the adopted nephew of Henry Rutgers. Rutgers (1745–1830), whose name you might recognize, especially if you live in New Jersey (or attended Rutgers University), was a native New Yorker and an American Revolutionary War hero. His family owned large tracts of land in Manhattan, including much of what is now the Lower East Side. After the war, Rutgers served in the New York State legislature and earned a reputation as a philanthropist.

He is credited with saving Queens College in New Jersey from insolvency in 1815 with a donation of $5,000. Ten years later, the name of the college was changed to Rutgers University, perhaps, according to some cynical sources, in the hope of benefiting further at the time of Henry's death. Instead, when Henry Rutgers died, unwed, in 1830, he left his fortune to the

Number 19 Crosby Street.

aforementioned William Crosby, who in turn became a philanthropist (and had a street, but not a university, named after him).

Two streets and a church on the Lower East Side were named for Henry Rutgers: Henry Street and Rutgers Street and the Rutgers Presbyterian Church. Incidentally, the Rutgers Presbyterian Church was originally

Numbers 134–40 Grand Street, at the corner of Crosby Street.

located on the corner of Henry and Rutgers Streets. Like Shearith Israel, it too moved uptown and has been on West Seventy-third Street since 1926.

And now let's get back to Crosby Street. In fact, we are going to retrace our steps along Crosby, going back a block or two until we get to Grand Street.

Right here on the corner is 19 Crosby Street (also known as 133 Grand Street). This building, dating from 1822, was part of a row of Federal-style homes that witnessed two centuries of changes in the neighborhood. Originally a residence, 19 Crosby Street became a carpentry shop in the 1850s as the neighborhood turned commercial. Not long afterward, the building was probably used as a brothel; records show that a number of men and women at that address were arrested in 1856 for "dancing and carousing in a noisy and disorderly manner." In later years, the ground floor was turned into a shop, and the upper stories were used for light industry, like many buildings in SoHo. Continuously in use for nearly two hundred years, the building currently houses a small food market.

And speaking of shopping, we are now heading west along Grand Street to where some of New York's luxurious retail emporia once made their home.

On the northwest corner of Grand and Broadway, where we stand looking at one of SoHo's many glass-and-steel luxury condo buildings, once stood a five-story white marble edifice, a cast-iron building that could almost have passed for an Italian Renaissance palace. This was the home of the Lord & Taylor department store during one of its several incarnations. One of the oldest department stores in New York City—though not the very first—Lord & Taylor had its origins on Catherine Street, a few blocks south of Canal Street. With a $1,000 loan from his

Lord & Taylor, Broadway, 1865. *Courtesy of Dover Publications, Inc.*

wife's uncle, twenty-three-year-old Samuel Lord opened a small dry goods store in 1826 and was soon in partnership with his wife's cousin, George Washington Taylor. Their business prospered, expanded and moved to ever-bigger premises until, in 1859, they established themselves on Grand Street and Broadway in one of the first of the great shopping palaces to arrive in SoHo.

Lord & Taylor prospered during the Civil War years, although it was reported that during the Draft Riots of 1863, the store armed its employees for protection against looters. (Imagine buying your linens from a gun-toting salesperson.) It was also in 1863 that Lord & Taylor opened a department known as "Mourning Millinery," an interesting detail in the history of merchandising. Its tenure on Grand and Broadway was relatively brief; it moved to the Ladies' Mile in 1870 and up to Fifth Avenue in 1903.

Sadly, the building that housed Lord & Taylor on Grand Street was destroyed by fire in 1967 and subsequently demolished.

Directly across the street, on the northeast corner, was another well-known department store; in fact, it predated Lord & Taylor by one year. This was Brooks Brothers, another retail giant with a long history.

Like Samuel Lord and George Washington Taylor, Henry Brooks and his brother started with a small shop on Catherine Street. They opened their first store in 1818, eight years before Samuel Lord's arrival on the same street. And like Lord & Taylor, Brooks Brothers moved uptown to Broadway forty years later, to another cast-iron confection that, like the Lord & Taylor building, no longer exists.

During their years on Catherine Street, Brooks Brothers' achievements included the introduction of the seersucker suit in 1830 and, fifteen years later, the first ready-to-wear men's suits. In 1849, Brooks Brothers clothed the men heading west to join the California gold rush, furnishing them with overalls, calico shirts and flannel underwear.

When Brooks Brothers opened its multi-story department store on Broadway and Grand Street, the store was described as "the most extensive and magnificent clothing house on either continent." The coat that Abraham Lincoln wore to his inauguration came from Brooks Brothers. When he was assassinated in 1865, he was wearing the same coat.

A somewhat more controversial story concerns the part Brooks Brothers may have played in the manufacturing of Civil War uniforms. Brooks Brothers was one of the suppliers of uniforms to the Union army. Perhaps due to the difficulty of providing so many uniforms at the same time—these were the early days of mass production—the uniforms produced were not always of the best quality. Brooks Brothers was, in fact, one of many companies trying to fill the needs of the army. And whether the poor quality of the soldiers' clothing and shoes was a deliberate attempt at profiteering or an unfortunate set of circumstances (insufficient supply of woolen material, inadequate machinery, too many soldiers, not enough time), the quality of the soldiers' equipment led to serious accusations. In fact, the word "shoddy" was coined at the time to describe the cloth used for the uniforms, which was said to be so poor that it would disintegrate in the rain.

But Brooks Brothers, like Lord & Taylor, survived the war and the economic depression that followed and soon moved north to its current midtown location, where in 1898 it introduced America to the button-down collar.

The fate of Brooks Brothers' fabulous cast-iron palace was also a sad one. Demolished not long after the department store left, another building soon replaced it. The building that stands here now, at 462 Broadway, was built in 1879 for another shopping emporium, Mills & Gibb, and is cited in the *AIA Guide to New York City* as a "mammoth cast-iron commercial palace [that]

Broadway and Grand Street.

evokes memories of the French Renaissance." Mills & Gibb, once a very successful lace and linen import company, has disappeared, and today we can find the International Culinary Center and its restaurant, L'École, at this address.

Walking a little farther south along Broadway, a short block beyond Grand Street, we come to Howard Street. Here on the corner is 434 Broadway, the location of the old Howard House Hotel, also known as Barnum's Hotel. It was here during the 1850s that three sisters from upstate New York attracted crowds of spectators to witness their powers as Spiritualists. The Fox sisters—Leah, Maggie (Margaret) and Kate—were perhaps the most famous mediums of the nineteenth century, with an international following that included Sir Arthur Conan Doyle, William Cullen Bryant and Horace Greeley. The popularity of their séances is considered one of the first significant landmarks in the history of the Spiritualist movement, which swept across America and England in the mid-nineteenth century and continued to attract adherents well into the twentieth century (nor has it disappeared in the twenty-first.)

The basis of Spiritualism is a belief in the possibility of communication with the dead. The Fox sisters, who began to conduct séances when two of the girls were still in their early teens, had an immediate following, communicating with the spirits through rapping, knocking and other preternatural means. After decades of success, the middle sister, Maggie, publicly confessed that these manifestations were done by trickery, shocking an audience of two thousand at the New York Academy of Music in 1888. The headline in the *New York Times* read, "Done with the Big Toe." The article described Margaret's confession and demonstration of how she and her sisters could crack their big toes to produce loud noises that were interpreted as rapping from beyond the grave.

Not everyone was convinced. Arthur Conan Doyle, for one, refused to accept her confession and continued his belief in Spiritualism (and, so it has been recorded, in fairies). One wonders what Sherlock Holmes's opinion of all this might have been.

One year later, the Fox sisters attempted to retract Maggie's public confession, but they were no longer considered credible. All three died in poverty and obscurity within the next few years.

Spiritualism, however, did not die out. The three million Spiritualists numbered in America in the 1860s more than doubled by the end of the century. Though Spiritualism gradually lost favor as a popular pastime, there is no doubt that it is still being practiced.

Number 434 Broadway, where Barnum's Hotel once stood.

Let's continue to the corner of Broadway and Canal Street. Across Canal—on the "wrong side" of the street (i.e., a few steps outside the border of SoHo)—and about a quarter of a block farther along is a location that we can't possibly pass without telling you its stories.

This was once the location of the Apollo Rooms, where, on December 7, 1842, the New York Philharmonic Orchestra gave its very first concert. Originally called the Philharmonic Society of New York, the orchestra was founded that same year by Ureli Corelli Hill, who, along with two other conductors, led the sixty-three-piece orchestra before an audience of six hundred. According to the *New York Times*, the members of the orchestra wore formal attire, including white gloves, and performed standing up (except for the cellos). The concert opened with Beethoven's Fifth Symphony, a work that was still relatively unknown. Tickets cost eighty-three cents.

The oldest orchestra in the United States, the New York Philharmonic has played continuously since 1842 and commemorated its 15,000th concert in 2010.

But that's not all that happened in the Apollo Rooms. It was here, in 1872, that the National Radical Reformers Convention was held and the Equal Rights Party was formed. The Equal Rights Party was the first to nominate a woman to run for the presidency of the United States. The candidate, Victoria Woodhull (1838–1927), was a notorious advocate of free love, birth control, divorce and women's rights.

Victoria Woodhull, like the Fox sisters, came of age at the dawn of the Spiritualist era and, before she had reached her teens, was on the road with her sister and her father, conducting séances, telling fortunes and selling patent medicines. When Victoria was twenty-two, the two sisters moved to New York and established themselves as "magnetic healers."

Woodhull's road from spiritual healer to presidential candidate was an interesting one. An early marriage led to divorce—which was highly frowned upon in the nineteenth century—followed by two other marriages. Along the way, Woodhull embraced and promoted the doctrine of free love and later became a spokesperson for women's suffrage. In fact, she ran for president fifty years before American women had the vote!

Victoria Woodhull and her sister, Tennessee, are credited with establishing the first Wall Street brokerage owned and operated by women and publishing their own weekly newspaper espousing radical social doctrines and exposing business and political inequalities and fraud. Their journal, moreover, was the first to print an English translation of the *Communist Manifesto*.

Along Crosby Street and Back to Grand Street

In 1877, Victoria Woodhull immigrated to England, where she spent the next fifty years, living long enough to see American women granted the right to vote but never actually exercising that right herself.

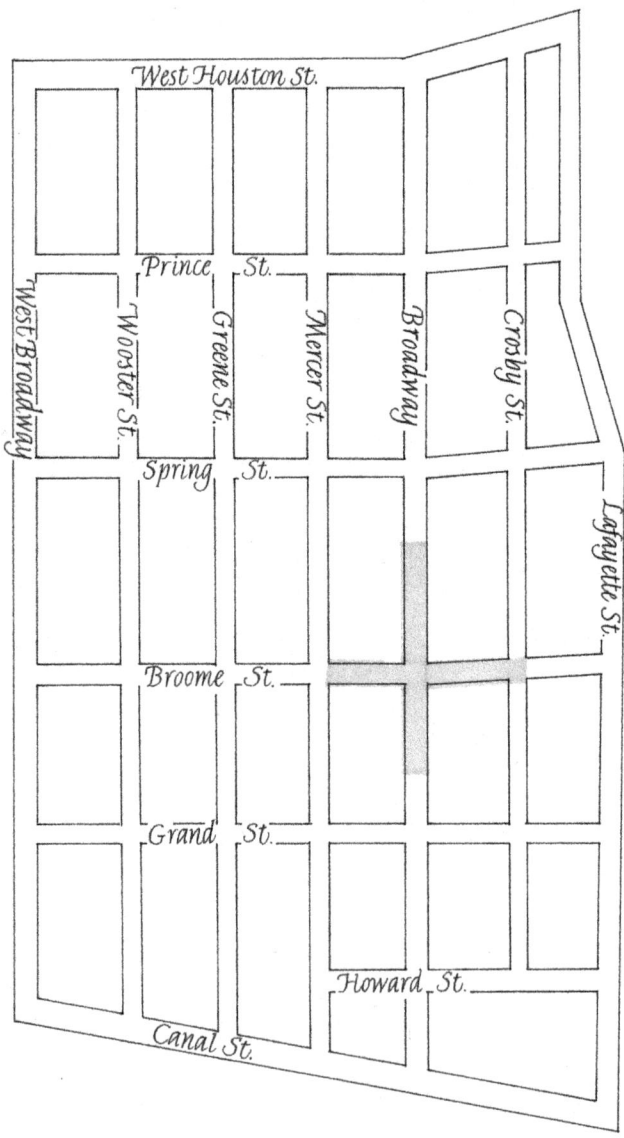

West Houston St.

Prince St.

West Broadway

Wooster St.

Greene St.

Mercer St.

Broadway

Crosby St.

Lafayette St.

Spring St.

Broome St.

Grand St.

Howard St.

Canal St.

5

Broadway and Broome Street

*Robert Moses's Folly, Jane Jacobs and Margot Gayle,
Daniel Badger and Richard Morris Hunt*

The corner of Broadway and Broome Street may not be the geographical center of SoHo, but it is an architectural and historical crossroads. Every direction boasts an imposing building, and the activity that swirls around us, at almost every hour of the day, is almost overwhelming.

Before we start sightseeing, let us introduce you to John Broome (1738–1810), a politician who served three times as lieutenant governor of New York State, from 1804 until 1810. A very successful merchant, Broome made his fortune by importing tea from China. His first shipment was said to weigh two million pounds. Broome was one of many who got rich trading with China. Another was John Jacob Astor, whom we'll meet in a later chapter. John Broome lived over his shop on Hanover Square, a couple miles south of the street that would one day bear his name.

Broome Street as we know it—home of magnificent, landmarked cast-iron buildings (among the best in the world)—once came close to being totally eliminated from New York City, and was the center of an urban development controversy that raged for nearly two decades. The cause of the conflict was Robert Moses's Lower Manhattan Expressway. Back in the 1960s, the threat of this roadway led community activists to do battle with city hall and the New York City Board of Estimates.

The original plan called for a ten-lane elevated highway that would cut across Manhattan, connecting the East River bridges (the Williamsburg and the Manhattan) with the Holland Tunnel on the west side of the island. And how would this be accomplished? By destroying fourteen

Broadway, looking north from Broome Street, 1866. *Courtesy of Dover Publications, Inc.*

blocks of buildings along Broome Street and Canal Street, a plan that would have displaced nearly two thousand families and more than eight hundred businesses.

Apart from the cost of $80 million, which had been approved by the Board of Estimates in 1960, the expressway would have meant the destruction of some of the finest examples of cast-iron (and other) architecture anywhere. The *AIA Guide to New York City* describes Broome Street between Broadway and West Broadway as "SoHo at its most idiosyncratic and hectic, a mixture of delightful cast-iron façades, previously decayed, now restored to glory." None of this would have survived had Robert Moses prevailed.

The movement to halt the construction of the Lower Manhattan Expressway was one of the great triumphs of Jane Jacobs. She and her organization, the Joint Committee to Stop the Lower Manhattan Expressway, fought valiantly for a number of years before the plan was finally abandoned in 1969. Jane Jacobs, an important figure in the history of New York City preservation, reportedly called Robert Moses's project "a monstrous and useless folly." As the key figure in a movement to save New York's neighborhoods, Jacob's march against the (almost) unyielding city government helped save large swaths of SoHo from the wrecker's ball.

Another woman whose name is inextricably linked with the history of SoHo and, more specifically, with the rescue of the SoHo cast-iron historic district, was Margot Gayle, an urban preservationist who died in 2008 at the age of one hundred.

Margot Gayle first came into prominence in the late '50s, when she and a group of neighbors met to discuss the erratic clock atop the tower of the Jefferson Market Courthouse in Greenwich Village. At that time, it had been stuck at 3:20 for two years. They formed the Committee of Neighbors to get the Clock on the Jefferson Market Courthouse Started. Their advocacy not only fixed the clock (well, temporarily) but also saved the entire building, which had been scheduled for demolition. The courthouse was transformed into the Jefferson Market Library in 1967.

That was not the only clock that Ms. Gayle saved—she was a founder of the Friends of the City's Historic Clocks—but her greatest achievement was the preservation of twenty-six blocks in SoHo (familiar to us as the SoHo Cast-Iron Historic District), which has been protected by the New York City Landmarks Preservation Commission since 1973. At the time of her death, the president of the Municipal Arts Society, Brendan Sexton, was quoted in the *New York Times* as saying, "Margot Gayle is the only reason we have a SoHo."

Founder of the Friends of Cast-Iron Architecture, Ms. Gayle was the author of *Cast-Iron Architecture in New York: A Photographic Survey* (with photographer Edmund Gillon Jr., published in 1974), an invaluable guide for lovers of architecture and walkers in the city. She also wrote *Cast-Iron Architecture in America: The Significance of James Bogardus*, with her daughter Carol Gayle; she was ninety when this book was published. (We made the acquaintance of James Bogardus in Chapter 3.)

Haughwout Building, 488 Broadway.

And speaking of cast-iron architecture, we are still standing here on the corner of Broadway and Broome Street. Right before our eyes is a marvel of the genre, the five-story Haughwout (pronounced How-it) Building, located at 488 Broadway. Called a "cast-iron magnificence" by the *AIA Guide*, this building has two fronts, one on Broadway and one on Broome Street, and ninety-two windows, all with curved arches and Corinthian columns. (Margot Gayle loved this building.) It has been compared to a Venetian Renaissance palazzo.

Built in 1856 (on land owned by one of John Jacob Astor's grandsons), Eder V. Haughwout took occupancy of the building in 1859 and opened his store, the E.V. Haughwout & Co. Store, where he sold top-notch china, glass, silverware and chandeliers. The store even marketed its own label of champagne. During the presidency of Abraham Lincoln, Haughwout & Co. supplied the White House with china, and the story goes that Mary Todd Lincoln never paid the bill. The Haughwout Store remained in this building for only ten years, but a century and a half later the building retains the name.

Broadway and Broome Street

Two significant features of the Haughwout Building bear mentioning: the cast-iron façade made by Daniel Badger and the revolutionary passenger elevator (more on that in a moment).

Daniel Badger (1806–1884) and his company, Architectural Iron Works, were major innovators in the history of architecture. As a pioneer in the use of cast iron as a building material, Badger literally changed the face of SoHo. (Why isn't there a Badger Street? Or one named after Margot Gayle?) In his youth, Badger worked as a blacksmith and later opened a foundry in Boston for the manufacture of wrought iron, which, as we mentioned in Chapter 2, was principally used for interior architectural details. It was in Boston that Badger took a risk and, in 1842, constructed one of the first all-iron storefronts, replacing the usual stone with iron. This may well have touched off the cast-iron architectural revolution.

Arriving in New York a few years later, Badger opened a small foundry in Lower Manhattan. The foundry was almost immediately successful, enabling Badger to move to a larger space uptown on Fourteenth Street and Avenue C, where he established his Architectural Iron Works Company. In *Cast-Iron Architecture in New York*, Margo Gayle wrote that Badger's company "turned out some of the most dramatic iron buildings this country has ever seen."

One of the most striking of Badger's buildings was the Haughwout Building. Not only did it house a very successful purveyor of luxury household goods, but it also boasted the first steam-powered passenger elevator in a public building, the invention of Elisha Graves Otis (1811–1861). A native of Vermont, Otis improved on existing elevator design by inventing an automatic safety brake that worked even if the power source failed. He presented it at the Crystal Palace Exposition in New York in 1854, calling his invention "an Improvement in Hoisting Apparatus Elevator Brake." His device could act automatically, in the event of a damaged or broken cable, to stop an elevator car from falling.

Following his success at the Crystal Palace, Otis founded the Otis Elevator Company in 1857. In 1861, he patented the steam elevator, the first of which had been installed a few years earlier at 488 Broadway, the Haughwout Building. Although Elisha Otis died shortly thereafter, his elevators—powered by electricity since the late nineteenth century—remain ubiquitous.

We are still standing on the northeast corner of Broadway and Broome Street. Before we move on, let's look diagonally across the street at 487 Broadway, located on the southwestern corner. This is another impressive building, built in 1895, twelve stories high, narrow and ornate. In fact, this

Broome Street, looking east toward Broadway.

almost-skyscraper benefited from Elisha Otis's elevators; buildings erected a few decades previously were limited in height by the number of stairs their occupants were willing or able to climb. The introduction of safe elevators changed that, ushering in the era of the skyscraper.

Apart from its imposing presence, this building is noteworthy as the address, in the early twentieth century, of the magazine *Casket*, "Devoted to the Higher Education of Funeral Directors and Embalmers."

Another of the nineteenth century's retail giants was to be found at this location, but not in the building that is currently standing. This was Rogers, Peet & Co., a department store established in 1874, when Marvin N. Rogers and Charles Bostwick Peet combined their two wholesale clothing businesses. Like many other clothing companies, they grew, expanded, opened a number of additional shops and ultimately went under in the 1980s.

Like Brooks Brothers, Rogers, Peet & Co. claimed credit for some marketing innovations; according to the company history, it was the first to label clothing with fabric composition and, rather more interestingly, the first to attach price tags to its garments—an innovation at a time when bargaining was still the norm.

The Roosevelt Building. *Watercolor by Leendert van der Pool.*

A further note about Rogers, Peet & Co. is that it used cartoons in its advertising—not a common practice 135 years ago—and one of its cartoonists was the young John Barrymore.

Almost directly across Broadway from Rogers, Peet & Co., we find ourselves in front of yet another architectural masterpiece, the Roosevelt Building, which is well known by architectural enthusiasts as one of the few remaining buildings in New York City designed by Richard Morris Hunt (1827–1895).

Hunt was probably the foremost American architect of the nineteenth century and certainly one of the most successful. The first American architect to graduate from the École des Beaux-Arts in Paris, Hunt introduced the United States to French architectural styles, especially the luxurious and flamboyant design of Renaissance chateaux. He made a name for himself as the "Architect of the Gilded Age," building vast palaces for the wealthy and powerful. One in particular, the Biltmore Estate in Asheville, North Carolina, had more than 250 rooms and required a specially constructed railway spur to transport materials and workers to the site while it was being built. The house was built for George Washington Vanderbilt, grandson of Cornelius Vanderbilt of New York Central Railroad fame.

(Interesting sidebar: Cornelius Vanderbilt was involved in the tale of Victoria Woodhull, whom you might remember from Chapter 4. Woodhull's sister, Tennessee, apparently used her clairvoyant powers to seduce Vanderbilt, who was then in his seventies [she was several decades younger]. Her intimacy with him helped the Woodhull sisters raise the money to start their brokerage business. But that's another tale.)

The house that Richard Morris Hunt built for Cornelius's grandson was set on grounds designed by Frederick Law Olmsted, a name with which many New Yorkers are familiar as the designer of Central Park.

Richard Morris Hunt built a number of mansions for the wealthy but also left his mark on public architecture, notably the design of the vast Fifth Avenue façade of the Metropolitan Museum of Art and the granite pedestal of the Statue of Liberty. His place in history was further ensured by his efforts in raising the status of architecture as a profession. Years before he built his famous mansions, he established the first architecture school in America and, in 1857, was a founding member of the American Institute of Architects (AIA). In fact, before the founding of the AIA, the term "architect" was appropriated by all kinds of craftsmen working in the building trades— masons, bricklayers and carpenters, among others. One of the founding principles of the AIA was "to elevate the standing of the profession."

The Roosevelt Building, which Hunt designed in 1873, has an interesting history. Although it was one of the later cast-iron buildings, it was one of the first that did not attempt to disguise the building material as stone. Many of the earlier cast-iron buildings were fashioned—and, in fact, painted—to give the appearance of masonry (stone). Hunt explored the revolutionary idea of allowing iron to look like iron.

The building, located at 478–482 Broadway, was originally built to raise funds for a hospital. It was erected in 1874 on the site of the home of James Henry Roosevelt, great uncle of Theodore Roosevelt. Upon his death in 1868, J.H. Roosevelt bequeathed his home and land to the Roosevelt Hospital, which built a commercial building (the Roosevelt Building) on the property in order to generate revenue. A five-story loft building, it was occupied from the start by the SoHo garment industry, which was beginning to flourish in the 1870s.

The Roosevelt Building was one of only two commercial buildings in New York credited to Richard Morris Hunt, and the other one, the New York Tribune Building, is long gone. The Tribune Building, erected in 1875, was demolished in 1955 to make way for traffic getting on and off the Brooklyn Bridge. It was one of the first real skyscrapers in New York, and its demolition is still mourned.

In 1898, three years after Richard Morris Hunt died, a monument was erected in his honor on the east side of Central Park. The sculptor who designed it, Daniel Chester French, is also credited with the imposing figure of Abraham Lincoln in the Lincoln Monument in Washington, D.C.

Let's walk back up the block, following Broadway past Broome Street. On the west side of the street, almost directly across Broadway from the Haughwout Building, is another building that's worth a look. This is the New Era Building at 495 Broadway, and it's especially attractive with its striking green mansard roof. Built in 1893, the design is a major departure from the Beaux-Arts style—i.e. the ornately appointed buildings that we've been looking at on Broadway and Broome Street. The *AIA Guide* calls it an "Art Nouveau marvel." The building extends right through from Broadway to Mercer Street and has entrances on both sides. Although originally built for the New Era Printing Company, the building was soon in use as the New York headquarters of Butler Brothers, one of the first mail-order catalogue companies in the United States. At the close of the nineteenth century, it had over 100,000 customers.

In the late 1920s, Butler Brothers created two franchises, the Ben Franklin Stores and Federated Chain Stores, both of which were very successful.

The New Era Building, with its mansard roof. *Watercolor by Leendert van der Pool.*

Number 502 Broadway.

Even during the Depression there were 2,600 Ben Franklin Stores and 1,400 Federated Stores around the country. By the mid-'60s, however, Butler Brothers was off the map, having sold its interest to larger corporations. But its name has not been forgotten. A recently renovated 500,000-square-foot, nine-story Butler Brothers warehouse in Minneapolis is located on Butler Square, the "Gateway to the Warehouse District." The Butler name is apparently still well known in Minnesota. And although the Ben Franklin Stores filed for bankruptcy in 1997, there are still Ben Franklin Stores in small towns across the United States.

Next door to the New Era Building—close your eyes and let your imagination soar—was once a vacant lot where, in 1838, the first giraffes ever seen in the United States were exhibited.

We are now ready to continue on our way, heading north along Broadway. In the middle of the block between Broome Street and Spring Street is 502 Broadway, the building where Harry Houdini worked as a teenager. What was Houdini doing here before he made his name as an escape artist? He was working as a stock clerk in a necktie factory. The company he worked for, H. Richter and Sons, made and sold ties, binding fringes and tassels during the SoHo garment district boom of the 1880s. It was Houdini's first job, and it was here that he met his first partner, Jacob Hyman; together they toured as the Brothers Houdini, hitting the music hall circuit and performing in Coney Island between 1891 and 1894. Houdini was all of fourteen when he worked in the necktie factory and seventeen when he launched his career as a magician and escapist, a career that brought him worldwide fame. His real name, by the way, was Erich Weiss (born Ehrich Weisz in Hungary), a name he changed in honor of his hero, the French magician Robert-Houdin, who is considered the father of modern magic. Houdini died at the age of fifty-one on Halloween 1926.

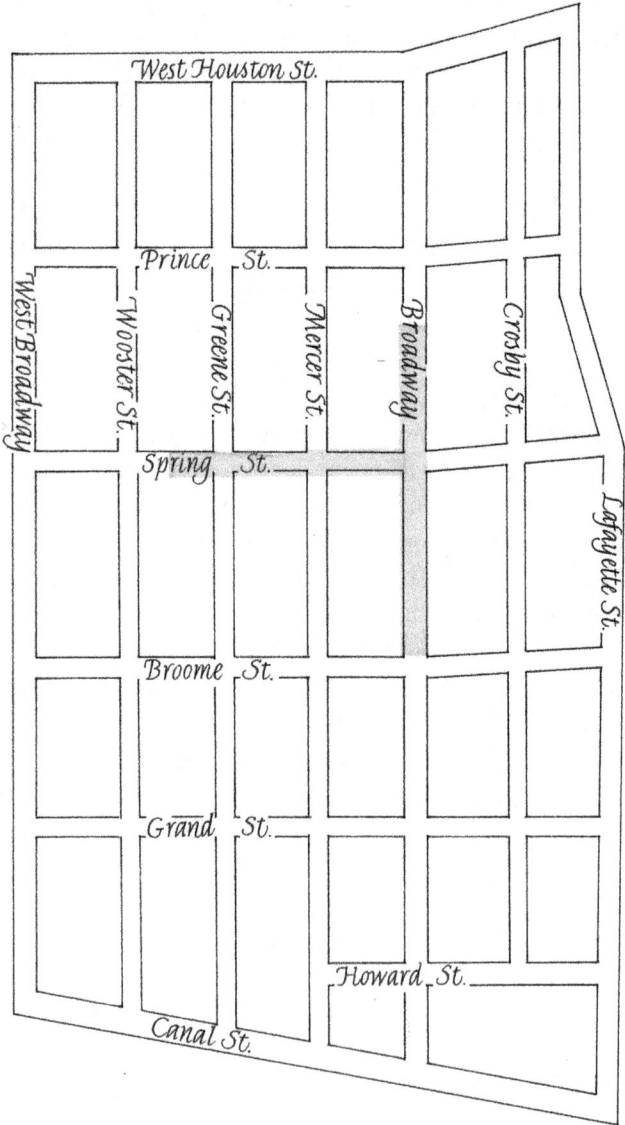

Broadway and Spring Street

Bishop's Crook Lampposts, the St. Nicholas Hotel,
Fernando Wood and the Copperhead Conspiracy,
the Ghost of SoHo and the Prince of Humbugs

We are walking along Broadway, heading north from Broome Street, on our way to Spring Street. There is a lot to see on these streets but also a lot that has disappeared.

Right in the middle of the block, on the west side of the street, is a beautiful old Bishop's Crook lamppost, a piece of New York history that one tends to walk past without a glance.

Did you know (did any of us know?) that there were seventy-six different types of lampposts in the city in 1934? (How do we know this? In 1934, the Department of Gas and Electricity issued a catalogue with photographs of the aforementioned seventy-six different lampposts.) Of these, only nineteen types remain, including three varieties of Bishop's Crooks lampposts. And one of them is outside 515 Broadway. These lampposts were installed around 1900, during the period when the New York Edison Company began replacing gaslight with electric light.

The lamppost we're looking at is one of the few of this type left in the city, although there is at least one other in this neighborhood, down the street on Broadway between Grand Street and Howard Street.

The reason there was such a variety of lampposts at the turn of the twentieth century is that no fewer than twenty-eight lighting companies were in business at that time, providing both the power and the equipment to illuminate the city. New York permitted a wide range of lamppost designs well into the 1920s.

Lamppost design took a tumble in the 1960s, when many of the historic cast-iron models were replaced by aluminum "cobra-head" posts,

Bishop's Crook lamppost on Broadway. *Watercolor by Leendert van der Pool.*

a decision that was not at all well received by the Friends of Cast-Iron Architecture. Subsequent efforts on their part, as well as by the Landmarks Preservation Commission, saved approximately one hundred original lampposts, including some in SoHo. Further efforts to preserve the style of these decorative models have resulted in the installation of numerous reproductions, most of which are based on the Bishop's Crook design. In fact, according to a Landmarks Preservation Commission report entitled *Historic Street Lampposts*, there are now far more reproduction lampposts than originals in New York.

As you walk through the streets of SoHo, you'll probably notice many lampposts that are very much like the one in front of 515 Broadway. How can you tell which are original and which are reproductions? It isn't all that easy. The originals have a small plaque, located somewhat above eye level, that reads, "Historic Landscape Preservation." It's the same color as the lamppost, so it's easy to miss. And the older lampposts are a bit more deteriorated than the newer ones, a little rusty and maybe not quite perpendicular to the sidewalk.

The Bishop's Crook lampposts, whether original or recently installed reproductions, add to the historic ambiance of these streets, especially at night, when they are lit by yellow, rather than white, light bulbs, casting a warm glow on the sidewalks and buildings.

The west side of Broadway between Broome Street and Spring Street also has another relic of the past: two buildings (521 and 523 Broadway) that are remnants of the marble façade of the once-glorious St. Nicholas Hotel.

Opened in 1853, the St. Nicholas was the preeminent hotel in New York City for most of its twenty-seven years of existence. A six-story marble edifice, it cost $1,200,000 to build and another $700,000 to furnish and equip, a vast sum of money in the mid-nineteenth century. The hotel boasted lavishly decorated accommodations for one thousand guests, a number of opulent public rooms and several dining rooms, one of which seated four hundred. Meal service was available nearly twenty-four hours per day—sounds like a cruise ship, doesn't it?

Central heating, hot and cold running water and one hundred suites with private bath and toilet facilities made the St. Nicholas the last word in luxury, and its own gasworks and fire department, located in the building, set it apart from other contemporary hotels. In addition to frescoed ceilings and walnut wainscoting, the St. Nicholas Hotel was lit by elegant gaslight chandeliers, which were furnished by the Haughwout & Co. Store, located, as we've already mentioned, on the corner of Broadway and Broome Street.

The remains of the St. Nicholas Hotel.

The St. Nicholas staff numbered between 250 and 400, depending on the season, and included 75 laundresses who washed and ironed six thousand pieces per day. Servants traveling with their employers were housed separately on the top floor and had their own dining room.

Although the St. Nicholas was immediately successful—and numbered several U.S. presidents among its guests—the hotel lasted only as long as the fleeting popularity of that part of Broadway. At one time New York's fashionable entertainment center, by the 1870s most theaters and pleasure palaces had moved uptown, and new hotels were built, accommodating the rich and powerful, as well as the ever-growing number of tourists visiting the city. The St. Nicholas closed its doors in 1884.

But the history of the St. Nicholas Hotel is not merely one of opulent rooms and sumptuous meals. It played a role in the history of the Civil War, specifically the Draft Riots of 1863, and more devastatingly, it became a target of the Copperhead Conspiracy a year later. Historians have written extensively about both of these events, so we'll be brief and mainly tell you about how the St. Nicholas Hotel featured in these stories.

The Draft Riots swept through New York City in July 1863, immediately after the U.S. Congress passed the National Conscription Act, which not only made the draft mandatory but also permitted government agents to

St. Nicholas Hotel, 1866. *Courtesy of Dover Publications, Inc.*

pick up young men in house-to-house searches. Even more egregiously, the law offered the rich the privilege of buying their way out of serving in the armed forces. The city erupted in violence. Fires were started, African Americans in particular were attacked, businesses were looted and destroyed and there was tremendous destruction of life and property during the four days before the riots ended. New York's mayor, George Opdyke, met with Union army general John Wool at army headquarters, which were located in the St. Nicholas Hotel, to try to figure out how to contain the riots, but they were unable to agree on a strategy. Although Opdyke, together with city police and Federal troops, is credited with ultimately suppressing the riots, he lost favor with New Yorkers and was advised not to run for reelection (he didn't).

The St. Nicholas Hotel figured even larger in the Copperhead Conspiracy, during which it was very nearly destroyed in a plot to burn down New York City. The story of the Copperheads is also the story of Fernando Wood (1812–1881), probably the most corrupt mayor in the history of New York. Elected four times between 1855 and 1862, he was accused of graft and patronage and, perhaps worse, of supporting the Confederacy during the Civil War. In fact, he headed a movement to promote the secession of New York City from the Union, which would have permitted profitable (for himself) commerce with the South during the war.

During his years in office, he was the center of a conflict between his chosen police force, the graft-ridden Municipal Police, and the Metropolitan Police, which had been created by the New York State legislature, resulting in the New York City Police Riot of 1857. Wood was arrested for corruption and bodily removed from city hall, but oddly enough, all charges were dropped. It was Fernando Wood's dishonest property finagling that forced the city to *sell* city hall at auction later the same year. The story is a bit complicated, but it involves the purchase of land by the city at greatly inflated prices, which would have earned Wood tens of thousands of dollars. When the city refused to pay the price, which apparently had been arranged by a legal transaction, the city hall building and its contents were sold. They were, fortunately, repurchased when the city was once again solvent.

We seem to be getting off the topic of the Copperhead Conspiracy. The Copperhead movement, with Fernando Wood as one of its leaders, arose among northern Democrats early in the Civil War. They were simultaneously antiwar, pro-Confederacy, anti-Lincoln and proslavery. Although pejoratively called Copperheads (after the deadly venomous snake) by members of the Republican Party, they proudly adopted the name in a more flattering sense, as representing the symbol of liberty on a copper penny.

Also known as the "Peace Democrats," the Copperheads joined forces with a group of Confederate army officers in a plot to destroy New York by starting fires simultaneously in a number of public places. Thirteen hotels along Broadway were targeted, as were other locations about which we shall soon read, including Barnum's American Museum and Niblo's Theatre, as well as docks, lumberyards and factories. The conspirators, who housed themselves in the St. Nicholas Hotel, figured that the fire department would not be able to fight all the fires at the same time. They were wrong. Many

Number 524 Broadway, Bayard Building, across from the St. Nicholas Hotel.

fires were indeed started, but the fire department was able to control them. Damage was estimated in the hundreds of thousands of dollars, including a considerable amount of destruction to the St. Nicholas Hotel. Although the conspirators planned to burn New York City to the ground and raise the Confederate flag above the ruins, they failed in their efforts.

As a matter of fact, history tells us that the Copperheads withdrew from the plot at the last moment, leaving the Confederate agents to do their worst. Most of the plotters escaped, and the St. Nicholas Hotel survived.

Across the street from the hotel, a theater known as Wood's Minstrel Hall was, at one time, located at number 514 Broadway. Opened in 1862 by Henry Wood—who just happened to be the brother of Fernando Wood— the 1,400-seat theater was one of several such establishments that flourished on Broadway in the middle of the century. Originally a venue for blackface minstrel shows, the name was changed to Wood's Theatre in 1866 in order to be perceived as a "legitimate" stage, and shortly thereafter it became the Theatre Comique. It was at the Theatre Comique that Harrigan and Hart produced and performed in their very popular musical comedies.

Although Wood's Minstrel Hall and the Theatre Comique may be forgotten, the partnership of Harrigan and Hart has a significant place in the history of musical theater. The two entertainers, Edward (Ned) Harrigan and Tony Hart, started performing together in the 1870s, specializing in music hall sketches lambasting the local militias and portraying the soldiers as drunken fools, to the delight of New York audiences. Their songs and comedy routines caught on, and the two men developed a string of very successful full-length musical comedies called the Mulligan Shows, considered to be the first shows of their kind in the United States. (In the late 1870s, Gilbert and Sullivan began their collaboration in Britain, although they may have appealed to a more sophisticated audience and probably would have preferred the word "operetta" to "musical comedy.") Harrigan and Hart purchased the Theatre Comique in 1876 and produced their Mulligan Shows there until 1881, when the building was demolished.

Henry Wood had another theater a block or so north of his Minstrel Hall. It was called Wood's Marble Hall, and it continued to specialize in blackface minstrel shows after the other theater became legitimate (or somewhat legitimate). Wood's Marble Hall lasted until 1877, by which time many of the SoHo Broadway venues had shared what was soon to be the fate of the St. Nicholas Hotel.

Before we continue up Broadway, we're going to turn left onto Spring Street and visit two locations with very colorful associations.

Broadway and Spring Street

One block from Broadway, on the north side of Spring Street, is number 91, the last home of Lorenzo Da Ponte (1749–1838), best known as the librettist of three of Mozart's most famous operas, *Don Giovanni, The Marriage of Figaro* and *Cosi fan tutti*. In fact, Da Ponte worked with Mozart during only a very brief period in a long and rather checkered career.

Born Jewish in a town near Venice, his family converted to Catholicism when he was fourteen, and ten years later Da Ponte was ordained as a Catholic priest. This in no way impeded his success with women. He had multiple love affairs and ran a brothel with one of his mistresses before fleeing to Vienna, just ahead of the police. Having been condemned by the Inquisition for writing seditious poetry, Da Ponte found a better climate in Vienna. It was there that he met Mozart, with whom he collaborated for five years, until Mozart's death in 1791. According to biographical sources, Da Ponte, still a priest, ran away once again, this time to Trieste with a married woman, and sometime thereafter to London, where he met and (perhaps) married a wealthy woman. Several years later, just before being arrested for debt, the two of them left Europe permanently and sailed to the United States.

Da Ponte's American career, begun in late middle life, included operating a distillery and a grocery store, managing a rooming house and a bookstore and ultimately landing a job—at the age of seventy-six—as the first professor of Italian at Columbia College in New York. He is also credited with introducing the work of Dante to America and organizing the first American production of *Don Giovanni*; he accomplished this when he was nearly eighty. And it was Da Ponte, well into his eighties, who opened and ran the first opera house in America, located in Greenwich Village. Lorenzo Da Ponte was still going strong when he died, here at 91 Spring Street, in his ninetieth year.

A block and a half farther along Spring Street, just on the other side of Greene Street, we come to a building that is said to be haunted by the Ghost of SoHo. This lurid tale of a young woman's murder is worthy of the tabloids, although it took place more than two hundred years ago. (In fact, it *was* taken up by the contemporary tabloids and referred to as the "Manhattan Well Murder.")

And here's what happened. On a cold, dark night in December 1799, a young woman named Gulielma Elmore Sands left her Greenwich Street boardinghouse (in what is now Tribeca) alone, presumably to meet her sweetheart, a young carpenter named Levi Weeks. She never returned. A few days later, two young boys saw a woman's scarf floating in a well in

Number 129 Spring Street, the location of the Ghost of SoHo.

Lispenard Meadow, right near where we are now standing on Spring Street. The police found Sands's drowned body in the well, and Weeks was arrested and charged with murder. Levi Weeks denied having been with Miss Sands on the night she disappeared, despite witnesses who swore to the contrary, and he was lucky enough to have as his defense attorneys none other than Aaron Burr and Alexander Hamilton (who had not yet fought their historic duel). Although popular sentiment was against Weeks, the jury acquitted him, and Weeks, very wisely, fled the city. The murder of Gulielma Sands was never solved.

Not long afterward, in 1817, a building was erected near where Sands's body had been discovered; number 129 Spring Street still stands and has been a restaurant for more than thirty years. The well, which was located about one hundred feet back from what is now Spring Street, was covered over many years ago but can still be seen in the basement of the restaurant. More than one person has reported sighting a ghostly figure clad in a robe of moss and seaweed, and other ghostly apparitions have appeared on Spring Street and in the streets nearby. Is Gulielma's ghost haunting Spring Street? There are those who say the answer is yes.

As we head back to Broadway, retracing our steps along Spring Street, be sure to cast a glance at number 107, the oldest building in SoHo. It was built at the very beginning of the nineteenth century, just after Miss Sands's sad demise. The building itself is not particularly distinguished; in fact, it's not interesting at all, except for its age. The *AIA Guide* doesn't mention it.

Let's continue along Broadway. We are now on the block between Spring Street and Prince Street. On the west side of the street, at 537–541 Broadway, is a fine cast-iron building, built in 1868, but we would like you to imagine a time just before this building was erected when this was the location of P.T. Barnum's American Museum, in its second incarnation.

The name P.T. Barnum is instantly recognizable to many Americans. Who hasn't heard of the Greatest Show on Earth? But Barnum did more than establish what is probably the world's most famous circus; he also entertained Americans for more than half a century.

Phineas Taylor Barnum (1810–1891), who has been called a master showman, the "Prince of Humbugs," and the "Shakespeare of Advertising," is actually hard to categorize. He was a brilliant entrepreneur and a consummate showman but also perhaps a liar and a charlatan. During his lifetime, he was one of the most famous Americans of the nineteenth century.

At the age of twenty-five, he kicked off his career by promoting Joice Heth, an elderly African American woman who claimed to be 161 years old and to have been George Washington's nurse. Exhibiting her at Niblo's Garden (on Broadway and Prince Street), he raked in $1,500 a week in admissions. According to the *New York Times*, he even sold tickets to her

The aftermath of the Barnum Museum fire, 1868. *Courtesy of Dover Publications, Inc.*

autopsy (which, if you think about it, is kind of hard to believe), at which time it was determined that her age had been somewhat exaggerated.

A few years later, in 1841, Barnum purchased Scudder's American Museum, an unsuccessful enterprise on Ann Street and Broadway in Lower Manhattan, which he transformed into an astonishing tourist attraction—a huge, five-story building crammed with artifacts, animate and inanimate, combining a zoo, a circus, magicians, minstrels, spectacles and panoramas (and a whole lot more). Among the exhibitions was an embalmed "mermaid" (the Feejee Mermaid) and General Tom Thumb, the twenty-five-inch midget who remained one of Barnum's star attractions for forty years. P.T. Barnum helped arrange Tom Thumb's wedding to Lavinia Warren Bump, one of the famous inhabitants of the St. Nicholas Hotel. During their honeymoon, they were invited to the White House to meet President and Mrs. Lincoln.

Wait, there's more. Barnum acted as impresario for the opera star Jenny Lind (the Swedish Nightingale), who was not yet known in America. His skill in advertising and marketing created what today would be called a media frenzy, with tens of thousands of fans fighting to purchase tickets to one of her ninety-five concerts—paying as much as $650, a price that was quite inconceivable in 1850. Barnum had never heard her sing before he organized her concerts; luckily for him, she was as good as he promised.

Barnum's American Museum on Ann Street was destroyed by fire in 1865, but Barnum was quick to relocate. His second American Museum opened the same year at 537 Broadway but lasted only three years before it, too, burned to the ground. By this time, Barnum was nearly sixty, but there was no stopping him. In 1874, he built a ten-thousand-seat arena on Madison Avenue and Twenty-sixth Street, in a location that would house the first Madison Square Garden a few years later. He called his arena Barnum's Great Roman Hippodrome, and it was here that he staged his first three-ring circuses, complete with wild animals, acrobats and, of course, the full panoply of exotica. He took his show on the road as "P.T. Barnum's Grand Traveling Museum, Menagerie, Caravan and Circus," which grossed $400,000 in its first year. In 1881, Barnum went into partnership with James A. Bailey, and Barnum and Bailey's Greatest Show on Earth was born.

A legend that has been perpetrated about Barnum is that he arranged for his obituary to be published before his death so he could enjoy reading about himself, but research indicates that this is apocryphal. He did, however, add two words to the language: *Barnumize* (not much used anymore), which means to trick or convince the public that something is much more spectacular than it is, and *jumbo*, in honor of the elephant that Barnum turned into a superstar.

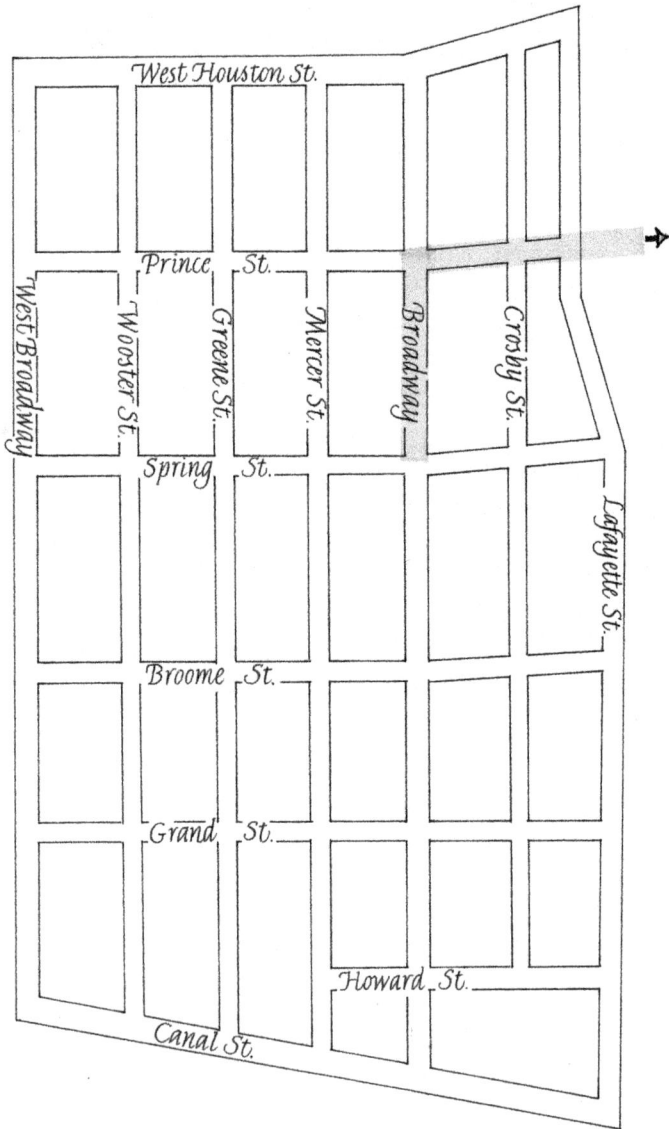

West Houston St.

Prince   St.

West Broadway

Wooster St.

Greene St.

Mercer St.

Broadway

Crosby St.

Lafayette St.

Spring   St.

Broome   St.

Grand   St.

Howard St.

Canal St.

7

STILL ON BROADWAY, HEADING FOR PRINCE STREET

The Free-Love League, Charles Broadway Rouss, Little Singer and Old St. Pat's

Having left P.T. Barnum (or his ghost) on the corner of Broadway and Spring Street, let's continue on our way past the one-time address of the New York Free-Love League to the Charles Broadway Rouss Building at 555 Broadway. If you look up, you can see his name stretched across the broad exterior of the building in huge, widely spaced letters.

But wait—perhaps you are wondering about the Free-Love League? It was part of a mid-nineteenth-century movement based on the principles of French philosopher Charles Fourier (1772–1837), and its doctrine called for allowing love (and passion) freer rein than contemporary mores permitted. A Utopian Socialist, Fourier's many treatises include much that is acceptable today—feminism, women's rights and the acceptance of social and sexual relationships outside marriage—but at the time he was considered very radical, and his followers were vilified.

Cooperative settlements, where work and personal lives were shared, were established on farmland in the United States and France based on Fourier's principles; these were, to some extent, similar to twentieth-century communes. The members of the New York Free-Love League were not part of an agricultural community, but they shared many of Fourier's beliefs. Among other precepts, Fourier believed that human passions should be indulged and that marriage was a form of slavery. Needless to say, this was not the most popular view in mid-nineteenth-century New York, and in October 1855, the headquarters of the New York Free-Love League at 555 Broadway were raided by the police and closed down.

The *New York Times*, in an article published a few years later, commented that the success of Fourier's philosophy resulted from "the proneness of mankind to commit wickedness" and called the members of the Free-Love League (who continued to flourish, despite the loss of their Broadway meeting place) "an ulcerous abomination of unrestrained lust." (Pretty harsh words from the *New York Times!*)

OK, back to Charles Broadway Rouss. The Rouss Building was built in 1890, thirty-five years after the Free-Lovers were driven out. A landmarked cast-iron and stone edifice, it housed the Charles Broadway Rouss Emporium, a vast department store whose motto was: "We shall keep everything calculated to make a man fashionable, a lady irresistible and a family comfortable."

Who was Charles Broadway Rouss and what was his real name? A self-made man, Rouss was the embodiment of the rags-to-riches-to-rags-to-riches American myth and was, in many ways, a legendary figure in New York City. Born Charles Baltzell Rouss in Maryland in 1836, he left school at fourteen, moved to Virginia and went to work in a shop, where he was paid one dollar per week plus board. He was able to save enough money to start his own business a few years later and continued to prosper for some years but lost everything at the end of the Civil War, having unwisely invested in Confederate bonds.

Rouss arrived in New York in 1866. Broke and homeless, he slept on park benches and sustained himself on free lunches. Thousands of dollars in debt, Rouss ended up in the Ludlow Street jail but somehow emerged to reinvent himself as a dealer in distressed merchandise (i.e., goods purchased cheaply from bankrupt wholesalers and resold at a large profit). Within a short time, he had turned his small business into a big one, and by the time he opened his emporium on Broadway, he was selling a dazzling array of luxury goods, everything from parlor organs to walking sticks, from jewelry to Japanese parasols and from carpets to corsets. Having fulfilled his vow to become a millionaire, Rouss changed his middle name to Broadway, in honor of the street where he had prospered.

Not overly modest, Rouss had a sign erected when his building was under construction. The sign read: "He who builds, owns, and will occupy this marvel of brick, iron, and granite, thirteen years ago walked these streets penniless and $50,000 in debt. Only to prove that the capitalists of to-day were poor men twenty years ago...Pluck, adorned with ambition, backed by honor bright, will always command success, even without the almighty dollar."

Numbers 123–25 Mercer Street, the Charles Broadway Rouss Emporium.

Rouss opened branches of his department store in Paris, Yokohama, Berlin, Vienna and Chemnitz and continued to prosper.

But in 1895, he went blind, and therein lies another tale. According to Rouss's obituary, he made a widely publicized offer of $1 million to anyone who could restore his sight. Not surprisingly, he was deluged with responses from doctors, healers, cranks and charlatans. He thereupon hired an impoverished blind man, paying him one dollar per day to test the many remedies that were being offered. Rouss's thinking may have been "If it works for him, it'll work for me" or "If it's harmful, let someone else take the risk!" Unfortunately, none of the remedies was effective, and Charles Broadway Rouss remained blind until his death in 1902. He was buried in Virginia in the largest private mausoleum in the United States, which closely resembles the Parthenon.

Across the street from the Rouss Building is 550 Broadway, an 1854 building with a cast-iron front that was added in 1901. This was once the home of Tiffany & Co., the world-renowned jewelry store. Established in 1837 in Lower Manhattan by Charles Lewis Tiffany and John Young, the shop was originally called Tiffany and Young. Not yet in the diamond business, Tiffany and Young sold stationery and other "fancy goods," which included buggy whips, canes and suits of armor. (One can only assume they were for decorative purposes.)

By the time they moved uptown to 550 Broadway, Charles Tiffany had become the sole proprietor, and the name was changed to Tiffany & Co. It was during the years at this location that Tiffany's began to specialize in gold and silver goods, as well as jewelry and gemstones. During the Civil War, Tiffany's also made swords for the Union army, including gem-encrusted presentation swords for Generals Sherman and Ulysses S. Grant.

Tiffany's remained at 550 Broadway until 1879 and then moved onward, first to Union Square, then to Thirty-seventh Street and Fifth Avenue and finally to Fifty-seventh and Fifth, its current location. Since the mid-nineteenth century, the name has been associated with the ultimate in luxury. The Tiffany diamond, which Charles Tiffany purchased in 1877, weighed 287.42 carats.

We are nearly at the corner of Broadway and Prince Street. Just one building south of Prince is an L-shaped edifice, with one façade on Broadway and one on Prince Street, wrapping itself around the corner building. And what a fine building this is. We are looking at the Little Singer Building, located at 561 Broadway (and 88 Prince Street), built in 1902 by Ernest Flagg (1857–1947) and praised in the *AIA Guide* as "a post-turn-of-the-century charmer."

At one time there were two Singer Buildings, the Singer Tower on Broadway and Liberty Street, about a mile south of where we are standing, and the Little Singer Building. The Little Singer was built first, followed six years later by the lamented Singer Tower, which was demolished in 1968. The forty-seven-story Singer Tower held the title of tallest building in the world for five years, to be replaced in 1913 by the Woolworth Building, which in turn was overtaken by the Chrysler Building in 1930 and the Empire State Building almost immediately thereafter.

The tale of Singer and his sewing machine is another entrepreneurial success story. Isaac Merritt Singer (1811–1875) was an itinerant actor who also happened to be a clever inventor. He did not invent the sewing machine—it had been around since 1790, and Elias Howe had taken out a U.S. patent in 1846—but Singer improved it by inventing the foot treadle. Singer was able to come to an agreement with Howe over patent rights and proceeded to open a small factory in a room over the New Haven Railroad Depot on Centre Street, just east of today's SoHo, where Singer sewing machine production began. Moving to a larger space, a six-story

The Little Singer Building.

building with a Daniel Badger cast-iron front, on Mott Street, I.M. Singer & Company increased production from 2,564 machines in 1856 to 13,000 four years later. (Singer was also said to have fathered eighteen illegitimate children, a busy man indeed.)

The Little Singer Building was his next move; it was constructed as a factory and office building for the company. Originally called the Singer

Manufacturing Company Building—it became known as the Little Singer Building when the downtown giant was erected—561 Broadway replaced Wood's Marble Hall, which you may recall from Chapter 6. Both façades are characterized by large, recessed windows, in front of which are wide, decorative, wrought-iron balconies stretching almost all the way across the front(s) of the building. Toward the top of the building is a large decorative arch with delicate wrought-iron curlicues that resemble the elaborate ironwork on the Eiffel Tower. This was not really a coincidence; Ernest Flagg was studying architecture in Paris at the time that the Eiffel Tower was completed.

Flagg himself was lucky enough to be the cousin of Cornelius Vanderbilt II. It was Vanderbilt who sent him off to the École des Beaux-Arts in 1888. Flagg returned to New York with French architectural views, which he combined with the flourishing American skyscraper technology. He married into the family of publisher Charles Scribner, who sponsored a number of building projects—mainly for himself—including the Charles Scribner's Sons Bookstore on Fifth Avenue and Forty-eighth Street. The bookstore closed in 1989 and has since been transformed into a clothing store and later a cosmetics shop. Flagg also built the Corcoran Gallery of Art in Washington, D.C., and the United States Naval Academy in Annapolis, Maryland. Like so many of SoHo's best buildings, the Little Singer Building has been converted into luxury apartments. A two-bedroom co-op apartment was advertised recently for $3,800,000 but could be rented for a mere $14,500 per month. There's no word at the moment as to its current availability.

And that brings us to the corner of Prince Street, named, according to one source, for "unidentified British royalty" (not very helpful). Laid out in 1797 and paved in 1809, Prince Street was at one time the terminus of New York City's very first railroad, the New York and Harlem Railroad, which began operation in November 1832. Its one-mile-long track stretched from Prince Street to Fourteenth Street and consisted of a single passenger coach pulled by horses.

The New York and Harlem Railroad expanded during the decades that followed and was purchased in 1864 by Cornelius Vanderbilt and combined with other New York train lines, ultimately forming the New York Central Railroad. It was Vanderbilt's grandson, Cornelius Vanderbilt II, who supported the young Ernest Flagg at the École des Beaux-Arts. He was also a patron of Richard Morris Hunt, who built Vanderbilt's enormous mansion in Newport, Rhode Island, to say nothing of George Washington

Vanderbilt's 250-room mansion in North Carolina. (The name Vanderbilt does keep cropping up. Remember Tennessee Woodhull? See Chapter 4 if you forgot about her connection to Vanderbilt.)

The New York and Harlem Railroad did not actually run through SoHo; rather, its track was several blocks to the east of Broadway, running along the Bowery.

If you pause momentarily on the northwest corner of Prince Street and Broadway, you might notice a piece of artwork that more preoccupied—or just faster—walkers could easily miss. Embedded in the sidewalk is Ken Hiratsuka's one-line sculpture, a six- by eight-foot carving consisting of a single continuous line that bends and turns along its granite surface without ever crossing itself. Hiratsuka (born in 1959) arrived in New York City from Japan in 1982 with a BA in sculpture. His two earliest public sculptures, the first in Brooklyn in 1982 and the second one here on Prince Street in 1984, were created surreptitiously, the artist working late at night with one eye out for the police. The Prince Street sidewalk took two years to complete and is signed: "Ken."

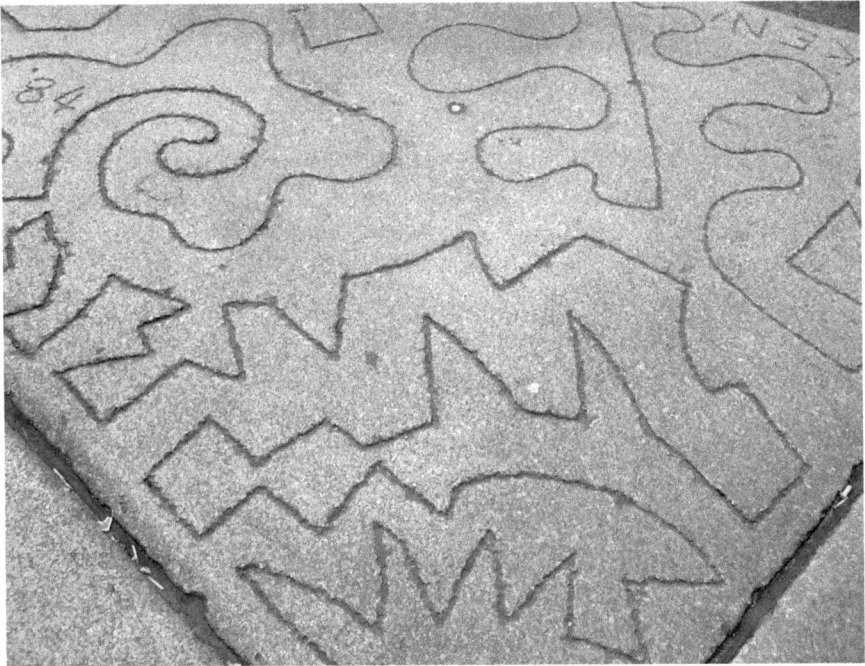

The Hiratsuka sidewalk sculpture at Prince Street and Broadway. *Courtesy of Leendert van der Pool.*

Hiratsuka's surfaces are often sidewalks, walls and rocks in their natural settings. Subsequent to his dark-of-night efforts in SoHo, Hiratsuka was recognized as an artist and won commissions in such far-flung locations as Australia, Brazil, China and the Gobi Desert, as well as Indonesia, Sweden and his native Japan. According to his website, Hiratsuka is continuing to carve "one continuous line in stone around the world," expressing "art's capacity to transcend the differences of nations and languages."

Before we push on and continue north along Broadway, let's turn right onto Prince Street and leave SoHo just long enough to visit Old Saint Patrick's Cathedral (now St. Patrick's Basilica), a block east of the Lafayette Street border of the SoHo Cast-Iron Historical District. Located at 260–64 Mulberry Street, between Prince Street and Houston Street, Old St. Pat's was the first Catholic church in the Archdiocese of New York. Built between 1809 and 1815 by the black French architect Joseph Mangin (who also built New York's city hall and worked on the Place de la Concorde in Paris), the church was enlarged twenty years later and, with a rapidly growing Catholic population in Manhattan, became a cathedral in 1850.

Old St. Pat's is steeped in history and has also played a role in popular culture. During the middle years of the nineteenth century, the Catholic population of New York was targeted by "nativists," white Protestant supremacists who were anti-immigrant, anti-Pope and rabidly anti-Catholic. The nativists, who considered themselves the legitimate, established inhabitants of the city, flourished in New York from 1830 through the 1850s. They particularly focused their hostility on the mostly poor and uneducated Irish immigrants who came to New York to escape starvation during the Potato Famine.

A staunch defender and protector of his Irish Catholic flock, John Hughes (1797–1864) became bishop of St. Patrick's Church in 1838 and first archbishop of New York twelve years later, when St. Patrick's became a cathedral. He was popularly known as "John Dagger Hughes" or "Dagger John," names that referred to the cross he drew next to his signature but also to his combative personality. When an anti-Catholic mob threatened to burn down St. Patrick's, Dagger John stood firm outside the building with his own mob of parishioners and members of the Ancient Order of Hibernians to defend the church.

Old St. Patrick's was, in fact, destroyed by fire in 1866 but rebuilt two years later. This was concurrent with the construction of the new St. Patrick's Cathedral on Fifth Avenue. When the new cathedral opened in 1879, St. Patrick's on Mulberry Street lost its status as a cathedral and

Old St. Patrick's Cathedral (now St. Patrick's Basilica).

returned to its original role as a parish church. And so it remained until 2010, when it became a basilica. (It was also designated a New York City landmark in 1966.)

Buried in St. Patrick's churchyard, behind high walls, was, until recently, Pierre Toussaint (1766–1853), the first African American slave to be proposed for sainthood. Toussaint was born into slavery in Haiti and was brought to New York by the Berard family, who owned him. Apprenticed by his master to a hairdresser, Toussaint proved to be very talented and was soon sought after by many wealthy New York women who valued his skill at creating the complicated and elaborate hairstyles that were then in vogue. A master hairdresser, Toussaint made quite a lot of money, which he invested wisely and profitably, and was soon a wealthy man.

When his master died, leaving a destitute widow and children, Toussaint took responsibility for the family and, still a slave, supported them on his earnings as a hairdresser. Upon the death of Madame Berard, Toussaint was granted his freedom; he was then in his early forties. A prosperous man and

Old St. Patrick's churchyard. *Watercolor by Leendert van der Pool.*

philanthropist, Toussaint spent the rest of his life doing acts of charity, caring for the poor and sick, establishing the first free school for black children in New York and contributing to the construction of St. Patrick's. He was also a founder of St. Vincent de Paul (the French Church, originally located on Canal Street).

Pierre Toussaint's remains were later moved to the crypt of St. Patrick's Cathedral on Fifth Avenue, the only layperson to be interred there. He has been a candidate for sainthood since 1991.

The unspoiled ambiance of St. Patrick's has attracted filmmakers and producers over the years. It is in the churchyard of Old St. Patrick's that Robert De Niro and Harvey Keitel converse in *Mean Streets*, Martin Scorsese's 1973 film. Scenes from *The Godfather* and *The Godfather Part III* were shot in the interior of the church. Martin Scorsese, incidentally, went to grammar school across the street from Old St. Patrick's.

The neighborhood surrounding St. Patrick's Basilica, once the center of New York's poor Irish community, has been known as Little Italy for the past one hundred years or so. Like a lot of New York City, it has been transformed in recent years to a trendy neighborhood of boutiques, up-market restaurants and cafés catering to the young and affluent. But St. Patrick's remains in place behind its high walls.

And we are now going back to SoHo to see what other ghosts are inhabiting Broadway.

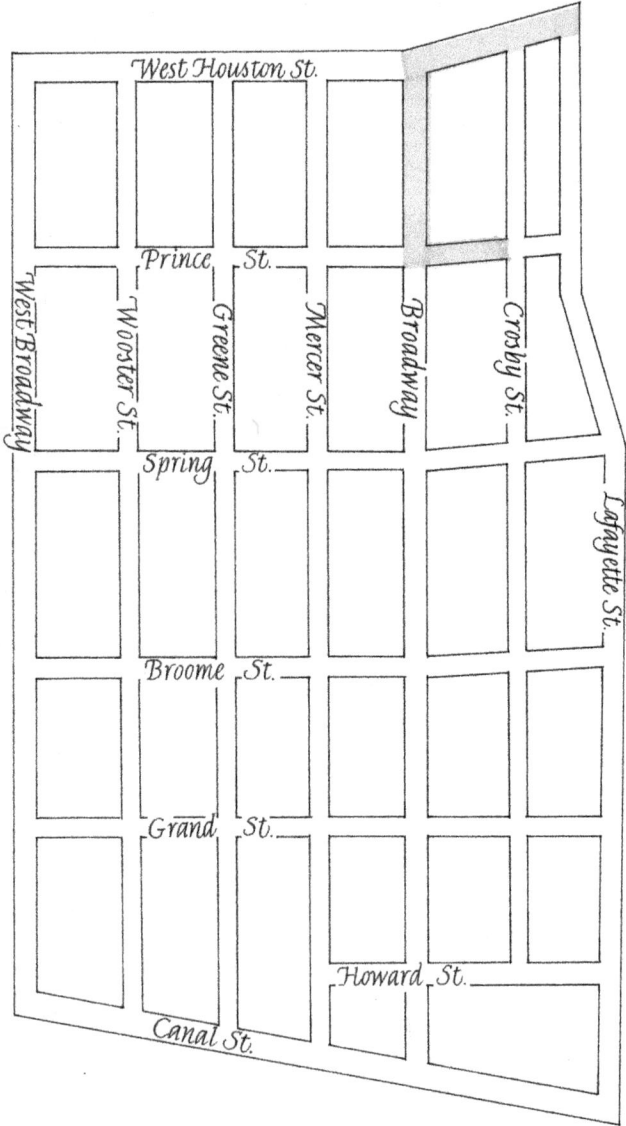

West Houston St.

Prince St.

West Broadway

Wooster St.

Greene St.

Mercer St.

Broadway

Crosby St.

Lafayette St.

Spring St.

Broome St.

Grand St.

Howard St.

Canal St.

8

BACK ON BROADWAY

Niblo's Garden, The Black Crook, *John Jacob Astor, the Comic Book Museum and* The Wall

Not so long after the consecration of St. Patrick's Church, a site was acquired by one William Niblo on the north side of Prince Street, extending from Broadway to Crosby Street. We are now walking right past there along Prince Street as we return from our brief foray into Little Italy.

Try to imagine this tract of land in 1828, when Niblo leased the property, which included a circus arena called the Stadium, used as a horse-training ground for the New York State Militia. He converted the arena into a theater, which he named the Sans Souci.

Niblo, born in Ireland in 1790, was an entrepreneur who made his first fortune as the proprietor of a coffeehouse (restaurant) on Pine Street in the Wall Street area of Lower Manhattan. When property became available on Prince Street and Broadway, Niblo was ready. He made his move at exactly the right time. The 1820s was the era of New York's great pleasure gardens. Predating the opening of Central Park by many decades, pleasure gardens were carefully landscaped parks (relatively small, compared to our current city parks), offering a variety of amusements: gardens, concerts, fountains and performances in indoor and outdoor theaters, as well as light refreshments. In the evenings, there were candle-lit paths to wander along, fireworks displays and other entertainments. A number of such gardens were designed, starting in the mid- to late eighteenth century, affording affluent New Yorkers the opportunity to eat ices, listen to music and flirt with one another. But none was as grand or as successful as Niblo's Garden.

A funeral parade, 1870, passing the Metropolitan Hotel and Niblo's Garden. *Courtesy of Dover Publications, Inc.*

When Niblo opened his venue, Prince Street was outside the city proper, so in his wisdom, he ran a private stage from the Battery to the door of his theater. In 1834, he rebuilt the small Sans Souci Theatre and changed the name to Niblo's Garden and Theatre, which soon became the place to go to escape from the city and have fun. In his three-story, three-thousand-seat theater, Niblo offered the public a wide variety of spectacle: pantomime, vaudeville, circuses with acrobats and tightrope dancers, concerts, plays and opera.

It was here at Niblo's Garden that P.T. Barnum launched his show business career in 1835 with his display of George Washington's 161-year-old nurse.

Two of the very interesting theatrical events that took place at Niblo's were the introduction of the Ravels to the New York public and, a number of years later, *The Black Crook*, which is considered by some to be the first real Broadway musical.

The Ravels, whom William Niblo first presented in 1836, were a French family of performers who were enormously successful in the very popular style of pantomime. The art of pantomime, which was a non-verbal—if not exactly silent—form of entertainment, combined skills associated with the circus, the theater and the ballet. Part clowning, part acrobatic feats in combination with lots of music and dance, pantomime was especially popular in the eighteenth and nineteenth centuries and was considered a lower-brow alternative to formal ballet, Shakespeare and other (more serious) legitimate theater.

The ten-member Ravel family was, from the start, very popular with New York audiences. Internationally famous for their acrobatics and high-wire feats, the Ravels returned to Niblo's annually for several decades; their shows were offered in alternation with productions such as *Hamlet, Macbeth* and *The Barber of Seville*. In 1857–58, the Ravels' show at Niblo's ran three hundred performances, filling the theater four times per week, a testament to their popularity and success.

A footnote to our mention of the Ravels concerns Leon Javelli, a one-time member of the troupe. Although not a Ravel by birth, his extraordinary skill as a high-wire dancer made him a great favorite; he was sometimes called "Leon Javelli Ravel." He died young, after performing in a show at Niblo's Garden, where, according to contemporary accounts, he supported five or six strong men, danced on the high wire and leaped over twelve soldiers brandishing bayonets. After the performance, he ate lobster salad and went for a swim in one of the New York rivers, where he seems to have drowned. The *Brooklyn Eagle* is quoted as saying, "Don't eat lobster salad. It isn't good, and besides, it is dangerous." To be fair, another account reports that he died of cholera, but whether lobster salad or cholera was the cause, Leon Javelli died in 1854 at the age of thirty-three. He is buried in Greenwood Cemetery in Brooklyn, as is William Niblo, who died at eighty-nine, twenty-four years after Javelli's tragic end.

By the time *The Black Crook* opened at Niblo's Theatre in 1866, Niblo himself had been retired for eight years. The story—though not the plot—of *The Black Crook* is part of musical theater history. Here's what happened: A troupe of French ballerinas was stranded in New York City when the venue where it was scheduled to perform, the Academy of Music, was destroyed by fire. William Wheatley, the manager of Niblo's Theatre, was shrewd enough to make a deal with the ballet company's producers to acquire the dancers, as well as their

Niblo's Theatre. *Watercolor by Leendert van der Pool.*

very elaborate sets and costumes, and combine all of this with the next play he was to produce. This happened to be *The Black Crook*, a fairly pedestrian melodrama involving evil forces, an innocent maiden, a noble youth and a pact with the devil.

He was successful. The play, written by Charles M. Barras, managed to incorporate all one hundred dancers, numerous irrelevant musical numbers and elaborate special effects. Despite its five-and-a-half-hour length, *The Black Crook* was the biggest hit ever at Niblo's, running for sixteen months at a time when theatrical productions typically lasted two or three weeks.

Why was *The Black Crook* such a success? Historians of the theater are quick to mention the chorus line of one hundred scantily clad dancers who appeared in flesh-colored tights and no doubt shocked and titillated the throngs of people who filled the theater during the play's 475-performance run. Condemnation for immorality on the part of the church and the press could only have increased ticket sales. (In fact, it's been conjectured that these stories were planted in the press by the theater in order to do just that.) One newspaper, in its description of the indecent costumes and dancing, compared Niblo's Theatre to Sodom and Gomorrah. The audiences couldn't get enough, and *The Black Crook*—although said to be totally without literary merit—toured for the next thirty years and earned millions of dollars.

Charles Barras, the playwright, incidentally, was not all that pleased that his serious drama was turned into a show business extravaganza. One account reported that the producers sweetened the deal for him—or perhaps purchased his acquiescence—with a generous payment.

But was *The Black Crook* really the first musical? That's a bit controversial. Music has been part of theater since ancient times (think of the Greeks), and *The Black* Crook, although it included an abundance of song and dance, did not particularly integrate the music with the plot. But it was certainly spectacular and was a major influence on Broadway theater in the years that followed.

In 1846 (twenty years before *The Black Crook* took Broadway by storm), William Niblo sold part of his property to the builders of the Metropolitan Hotel, which was erected at the corner of Broadway and Prince Street a few years later. The Metropolitan was soon in competition with the St. Nicholas, attracting the rich and socially connected to New York's fashionable shopping and entertainment district. Niblo's Garden extended from the back of the hotel to Crosby Street, but entrance to Niblo's Theatre could also be gained through the hotel itself. The Metropolitan Hotel, which lasted only thirty years, boasted "sky parlors," where ladies could look down on the Broadway parade without actually being seen (or jostled) themselves.

Half a block north of the Metropolitan Hotel and on the other side of the street stood Stanwix Hall in the mid-nineteenth century. Although long gone, Stanwix Hall—a bar and dance hall—merits a note in the history books as the place where Bill "the Butcher" Poole was fatally shot in 1855. Bill the Butcher had a colorful career that was glamorized somewhat in the movie *Gangs of New York*. A nativist and leader of the Know-Nothing Party (not a name to be proud of), Poole was a thug and a bad guy who probably merited—and certainly provoked—his violent end.

Next door to the site of Stanwix Hall is the Astor Building, built in 1896–1897 and adorned with Corinthian columns. But more interesting than the current building was what came before: the mansion where John Jacob Astor (1763–1848), at one time the wealthiest man in America and one of the richest men in the world, spent the last seventeen years of his life.

Astor, born Johann Jakob Astor in Walldorf, Germany, came to the United States at the age of twenty, and quickly established himself in the fur trade. By the time he was thirty, he was the most important fur merchant in the United States, dealing first with Europe and later with China, where he traded furs for tea and silk. By 1808, he was the first American millionaire.

Astor was a visionary. Predicting a great future for New York City, he started buying land as early as 1789 and, having profited magnificently on trade with China, purchased large tracts of land in Manhattan and north of the city line. This included, in 1803 and 1804, Richmond Hill, the estate of Aaron Burr, who was not only strapped for cash but also in need of a quick exit from the city following his duel with Alexander Hamilton. Astor also made a large profit buying government bonds wholesale (during the War of 1812) and selling them retail.

His property holdings included large parcels of land in Greenwich Village, as well as north and west of what is now SoHo. In 1798, he leased some of his land to a Frenchman named Delacroix to build Vauxhall Gardens, a pleasure garden that predated Niblo's by more than twenty-five years. Later, when the area was paved and streets were laid, Astor Place was one of the streets that replaced Vauxhall Gardens.

By 1830, Astor had left the fur and tea trade completely and was invested heavily in New York real estate. In 1836, he built the city's most opulent hotel—the Park Hotel, later renamed (guess what?) the Astor House—on Broadway and Fulton Street, near city hall. The Park Hotel, which had three hundred rooms, was surpassed twenty years later by the St. Nicholas, which had six hundred.

John Jacob Astor's real estate profits in Manhattan were legendary. He was quoted as saying, at the end of his life, "Could I begin life again, knowing what I now know, and had money to invest, I would buy every foot of land on the Island of Manhattan." A powerful and ruthless landlord who foreclosed mercilessly on tenants who failed to pay their mortgages, Astor also had his hand in banking, railroads, insurance and the entertainment business. He was well respected, if not well loved.

When Astor died in 1848, right here in his mansion at 583 Broadway, he left the bulk of his fortune to his son William Backhouse Astor, who doubled it and, when he in turn died in 1875, bequeathed $40 million to his own two heirs. John Jacob Astor's will also provided $400,000 to establish the Astor Library, a free public reference library. Astor's bequest led to the founding of the New York Public Library, which was established in 1895. (The rest of the money, actually the bulk of it, came from Samuel J. Tilden).

Today, the Astor Mansion is gone, as are the Astor House Hotel and Vauxhall Gardens. Astor Place remains, as does the Waldorf-Astoria Hotel, named after Astor and the town where he was born. John Jacob Astor actually had nothing to do with the Waldorf-Astoria; it was built by his descendants fifty years after his death. The current Waldorf-Astoria on Park Avenue is the second hotel of that name. The original was a consolidation of two adjacent hotels located on Fifth Avenue and Thirty-third Street: the Waldorf and the

Astoria, built in 1893 and 1897, respectively. They were torn down in 1929 to make way for the Empire State Building. Astoria, Queens, however, was named in John Jacob Astor's honor.

Well after Astor's death, the property adjacent to where the Astor Mansion had been located was used for the building that housed the New Museum of Contemporary Art, but it too moved on, relocating in 2007 to a large and impressive building at 235 Bowery.

A much smaller museum, however, can be found on the east side of the street, on the fourth floor of 594 Broadway. This is the Museum of Comic and Cartoon Art, also known as MoCCA. Established in 2001 in the back of a frame shop on Union Square, MoCCA now occupies a three-thousand-square-foot space. According to its website, the museum preserves and displays every form of comic and cartoon art: "animation, anime, cartoons, comic books, comic strips, gag cartoons, humorous illustration, illustration, political illustration, editorial cartoons, caricature, graphic novels, sports cartoons, and computer-generated art."

MoCCA hosts its MoCCA Fest each year, a popular fundraising event featuring exhibitions, panel discussions and interviews, where the annual Klein Award is presented, named for MoCCA's founder, Lawrence Klein. Among the recipients have been Jules Feiffer, Art Spiegelman and Roz Chast.

New York has always been a fertile ground for cartoon and comic book creation and has dozens of comic book stores but only one comic art museum (and here it is in SoHo).

In the mid-nineteenth century, two theaters, the Empire and the Santa Claus, were located at 596 Broadway, next door to the building that houses MoCCA, but neither lasted very long or made much of a mark on theatrical history. The building, however, is notable for being the one-time studio of sculptor Jonathan Scott Hartley, where America's oldest artists' club was founded in 1871. This was—and still is—the Salmagundi Club, which has had its home in a landmarked brownstone on Fifth Avenue and Eleventh Street since 1917. But in the years following its inception, the club was homeless. Originally an artists' sketch group, it moved from studio to studio, relying on the hospitality of its members for nearly thirty years.

The club changed its name twice (first calling itself the New York Sketch Class and then the New York Sketch Club) between 1871 and 1877, when it adopted its somewhat unusual name. Two theories have been suggested: one, that the name was borrowed from Washington Irving's *Salmagundi Papers*, and two, that the club named itself after salmagundi stew, a dish with a variety of ingredients (still served in the club's dining room).

The Salmagundi Club has flourished for well over 140 years. With a membership roll of over eight hundred, it has remained a bastion of figurative (i.e., representational) art through the eras of abstract expressionism, pop art, conceptual art and installations. It has numbered among its members many of the bright lights of American art history, including Childe Hassam, N.C. Wyeth and Louis Comfort Tiffany (of Tiffany Glass fame, son of Charles, whom we met in Chapter 6). Norman Rockwell was also a member, as was Stanford White, although his profession as architect almost got him blackballed. Winston Churchill became an honorary member in 1958.

We are getting very close to Houston Street, the northern border of SoHo. On the southwest corner of Broadway and Houston is a piece of artwork that would never have been welcome in the Salmagundi Club (nor would it have fit). Officially titled *The Wall*, it is sometimes called the "Gateway to SoHo," and it is a very large installation occupying much of the north wall of 599 Broadway, facing Houston Street.

The artist, Forrest Myers, who calls himself "Frosty," was an early member of SoHo's artist community in the 1960s. He was commissioned to create *The Wall* in 1973 by a group called City Walls, for which he received $1,500. The artwork consists of forty-two turquoise aluminum beams attached to—and extending from—a bright blue wall, six rows across and seven down, covering a surface that is seven stories high and nearly as wide. In 1977, the owner of the building applied for a permit to have it removed, in order to use the space for advertising. A lengthy court battle ensued, and in 2002, *The Wall* was put into storage. With some assistance from the Landmarks Preservation Commission, a compromise was reached, and *The Wall* was reinstalled in 2007, positioned eighteen feet higher than originally to allow space for street-level advertising.

Exhausted by years of litigation, the artist made a statement to the *New York Times* in 2007: "If I had to do it over again, I would not do this, I would not do another public artwork. I would not encourage anybody to do a public artwork." Frosty moved out of SoHo in 1986, but *The Wall* is solidly in place right here at the end—or the beginning—of SoHo.

Houston Street divides SoHo from Greenwich Village. A wide thoroughfare, it extends from river to river, calling itself West Houston Street from the Hudson to the west side of Broadway and East Houston from the other side of Broadway to the East River. (Most New Yorkers, however, just call the whole street Houston Street.)

Houston Street was originally cut through the estate of Nicholas Bayard, who at one time was the largest landowner in Manhattan (a long time before

The Wall, sculpture by Forrest Myers.

Astor). The street was named for a lawyer from Georgia, William Houstoun (1755–1813), who married into the Bayard family. Houstoun was a delegate to the Constitutional Convention in 1787 and one of the few who refused to ratify it. When Houston Street was named in the early 1800s, it was William Houstoun's family connections, rather than his political record, that won him the distinction of having the street named for him.

A couple blocks east of Broadway on Houston Street is a building that straddles the borders of SoHo and Little Italy. This is the Puck Building, which extends from Lafayette Street (in SoHo) to Mulberry Street (in Little Italy), and it is very impressive. When the building was originally constructed in 1885–86, the west side extended into what is now Lafayette Street. Then, a few years later, Lafayette Street was widened and extended, which necessitated demolishing the entire west side of the building and adding a new façade. (In fact, Lafayette Street didn't exist then; it was called Elm Place. The name was changed when the street was extended.) The new façade was installed in 1894, and it is here, directly over the main door of the building, that one of the two large gilded figures of Puck presides over Lafayette Street. The other, even larger statue of Puck is three stories up, at the Houston and Mulberry Streets corner of the building.

The statue of Puck
on the façade of
the Puck Building.
*Watercolor by Leendert
van der Pool.*

Puck, the impish sprite from *A Midsummer Night's Dream*, adorns the building because it was originally built for the publishers and printers of *Puck* magazine. A satirical political magazine, *Puck* was a groundbreaker in a number of ways. Originally created in 1870 by an Austrian immigrant, Joseph Keppler, *Puck* was first published in German. In 1877, an English edition appeared, and for a few years, *Puck* was published in both languages; around the turn of the century, the German edition disappeared.

Puck magazine was characterized not only by its sharp wit and outspoken point of view but also by its beautifully rendered cartoons, which—unusual

The Puck Building, Mulberry Street façade.

for the late nineteenth century—were printed in color. When the magazine first appeared, Keppler was the only cartoonist, but as it grew in popularity, he hired a staff of artists and illustrators.

The weekly magazine, which took a stand against women's suffrage, trade unions and the Catholic church, also mocked the white male capitalists and corrupt machine politicians who were, the editors believed, running the country. *Puck* magazine was wildly popular, attracting nearly ninety thousand subscribers at its peak in the 1890s. By 1917, however, *Puck* had lost popularity; it ceased publication in 1918, not long after being purchased by William Randolph Hearst, one of the white male capitalists whom the magazine had mocked.

Puck magazine was headquartered in this gigantic building from 1887 until the magazine's demise. For decades thereafter, the Puck Building held numerous printing companies, as well as typesetters and ink manufacturers.

Today, the illustrations from *Puck* magazine are highly valued and are included in museum collections. It is interesting to note that the Museum of Cartoon and Comic Art's annual MoCCA Fest was held in the Puck Building for the first seven years of the museum's existence.

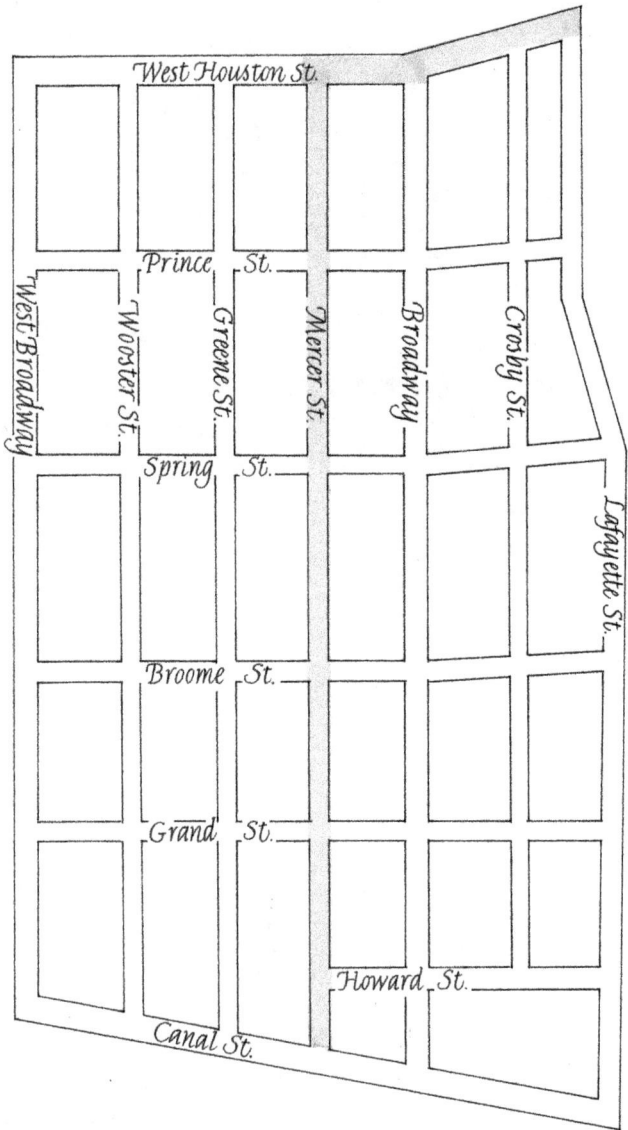

9

Along Houston to Mercer Street

The Cable Building, Fanelli's Café, Artists and Brothels

L et's walk back along Houston Street from the Puck Building and stop once again on the corner of Broadway and Houston. On the north side of the street, directly across Houston Street from *The Wall*, is a beautiful building with a very interesting history.

The Cable Building at 611 Broadway is an eight-story Beaux-Arts structure extending from Broadway to Mercer Street. It was built in 1893 by the architectural firm of McKim, Mead and White as the center of operations for the large and unwieldy surface transportation system that served New York in the late nineteenth century.

At that time, a number of rival companies provided public transportation, including elevated train lines, surface railroads and horse-drawn streetcars, to New York's population. Disorganized, badly maintained and poorly managed, the streetcar system was badly in need of rehabilitation when a group of wealthy businessmen created the New York Cable Railway Company, a syndicate established with the aim of consolidating and controlling surface transportation. Their plan was to introduce steam-powered cable cars to replace the horse-drawn vehicles and to buy, or otherwise acquire, as many of their competitors as possible.

The New York Cable Railroad Company and its subsidy, the Broadway Cable Company, were able to secure the resources to install cable lines under Broadway and to build the Cable Building to house the machinery that would control the lines. The Cable Building consisted of office and commercial space above ground; in the basement of the building were steam engines and wheels

The Cable Building, at Broadway and Houston Street.

measuring twenty-six feet in diameter that controlled steel cables installed just beneath the surface of Broadway. The cable cars ran along tracks that covered an area extending from the bottom of Manhattan to Thirty-sixth Street.

The construction of the Cable Building cost the syndicate $750,000, and the underground cable machinery cost $12 million. Unfortunately, the system did not work very well. Frequent accidents occurred that shut down the entire streetcar system, and the forty-ton cables, which tended to break, were difficult to replace. To make matters worse, the steam-powered cable technology was very quickly replaced by cheaper and safer electrical power. In 1901, the Broadway Cable Co. went bankrupt, the last steam-powered cable cars were discontinued, and the entire operation at 611 Broadway was shut down.

The cable equipment was removed from the basement of 611 Broadway a long time ago, but the building is still called the Cable Building. A commercial building, it has not—as far as we know—been turned into condos.

It's hard to mention the architectural firm of McKim, Mead and White without telling the lurid, if not entirely unfamiliar, tale of Stanford White and the "Girl in the Red Velvet Swing."

At the turn of the twentieth century, McKim, Mead and White was the most important architectural firm in the United States, with commissions

The entrance to the Cable Building, with its original logo. *Watercolor by Leendert van der Pool.*

that ranged from millionaires' country homes to the Municipal Building on Centre Street and the Washington Square Arch. Stanford White (1853–1906) went into partnership with Charles McKim and William Mead in 1879 and was considered by many to be the creative force in the firm.

White was a man of appetites, among which was a taste for young (very young) girls and wild parties. Although married, he maintained a separate apartment on West Twenty-fourth Street for romantic trysts, decorated, we have been told, with mirrored walls, plush couches and a red velvet swing hanging from the gold-leaf ceiling, upon which his young guests would entertain him.

None of this would be terribly interesting more than one hundred years after White's death had he not taken up with a sixteen-year-old chorus girl named Evelyn Nesbitt, who was more than thirty years his junior. What ensued is a well-known tale, thanks to E.L. Doctorow's 1970 novel, *Ragtime*, and the film and Broadway musical of the same name, adapted from the book. (There was also a film, *The Girl in the Red Velvet Swing*, starring Ray Milland, Joan Collins and Farley Granger, which was released in 1955.)

Stanford White and Evelyn Nesbitt had a brief affair that ended when Nesbitt was seventeen. A few years later, she married a cruel and jealous millionaire named Harry K. Thaw. Obsessed with his wife's amorous history, Thaw confronted White at a performance of *Mam'zelle Champagne* in the rooftop supper club of Madison Square Garden. While the chorus sang "I Could Love a Million Girls," Thaw shot White three times in the head. Thaw was heard to say either: "You ruined my wife" or "You ruined my life." White died instantly, and the subsequent arrest and murder trial of Thaw captured the attention of the masses. It was the contemporary press that first called Nesbitt the "Girl in the Red Velvet Swing." Although Thaw was convicted of murder, he was found guilty by reason of insanity, the first time that the insanity plea was successfully invoked in the United States. Thaw spent less than ten years in Matteawan State Hospital for the Criminally Insane and divorced Nesbitt upon his release in 1917.

It's a pretty racy story but would probably have disappeared without a trace had White not been a famous architect (and bon vivant), had Thaw not been a multi-millionaire and had Evelyn Nesbitt not been a famous—perhaps infamous—beauty.

Somewhat ironically, Madison Square Garden, the building in which Harry Thaw shot Stanford White, had been designed by McKim, Mead and White. (In fact, the building had also been financed by White, along with J.P. Morgan and Andrew Carnegie.)

The Cable Building, by the way, was built on the site of St. Thomas's Church, which stood on the corner of Broadway and Houston Street from 1826 until 1870, when it moved to its current location on Fifth Avenue and Fifty-third Street. The original St. Thomas's was attended by the Astor family. John Jacob Astor's son and heir, William Backhouse Astor, was one of the founders of the church, and John Jacob himself was entombed at St. Thomas's in 1848. When St. Thomas's moved uptown, Astor's remains were relocated to the Astor family vault at Trinity Church Cemetery in the northern reaches of Manhattan.

It's time to cross Houston Street and return to Soho. (The Cable Building is technically across the borderline. But we won't let that get in the way of a good story.)

Walking one block west along Houston Street, we come to Mercer Street, which runs parallel to Broadway. The street was named for a Revolutionary War general, Hugh Mercer, who died at the Battle of Princeton in 1777. We're going to turn left and head south along Mercer Street in the direction of Prince Street, passing New York's last volunteer firehouse, the Firemen's Hall, built in 1854, at a time when many of New York's firefighters were

St. Thomas's Church, a nineteenth-century view. *Watercolor by Leendert van der Pool.*

volunteers. In 1865, the New York State legislature passed a law abolishing volunteer fire departments and creating the state-controlled Metropolitan Fire Department. Five years later, the city took over, and the Fire Department of the City of New York (FDNY), was established.

Firemen's Hall was later converted to New York City Fire Department Hook and Ladder Co. #20. Unfortunately, the decorative architectural detail that once enhanced the building's façade has been removed. The building is notable today for having been a hangout of Walt Whitman.

The corner building, 99 Prince Street, used to be the address of the Astor fur coat factory, but we are going to walk right past it, cross the street and head for Fanelli's Café, one of the oldest bars in New York. Located at 94 Prince Street on the southwest corner of Prince and Mercer, the building housing Fanelli's was built in 1857 on land that was once part of Nicholas Bayard's farm (like much of SoHo and Greenwich Village). It was originally a grocery store, but like other nineteenth-century groceries, it offered beer and liquor for sale and gradually evolved from corner grocery to corner saloon.

Between 1878 and 1902, the building at 94 Prince Street was leased to Nicholas Gerdes, whose name still appears over the front door and whose operating licenses still hang on the wall. Michael Fanelli purchased the bar in 1922, which coincided with Prohibition, during which time Fanelli's operated as a speakeasy, serving homemade beer and wine and bootleg liquor. The Fanelli family kept the bar in business throughout Prohibition and well into the 1980s, when the bar changed hands. The name, however, remains unchanged, and the atmosphere offers us a welcome break from the constant throngs on SoHo's busy streets.

Two other bars currently in business predate Fanelli's: the Bridge Café on Water Street, which opened in 1847 and is the oldest bar occupying the same building in New York City, and Pete's Tavern on Irving Place, opened in 1857, where O'Henry (among others) used to drink. Fanelli's is the third-oldest bar in the city and the oldest in SoHo.

In the mid-nineteenth century, this side of Mercer Street was lined with expensive brothels all the way from Houston Street to Canal Street. In fact, the brothels were not only on Mercer Street but on Greene and Wooster Streets as well. All three streets run parallel to Broadway, where the grand hotels, theaters and pleasure gardens were located and potential customers abounded.

Prostitutes were available all over the city, but the SoHo brothels were, at that time, among the best in town. Lavishly furnished and

Along Houston to Mercer Street

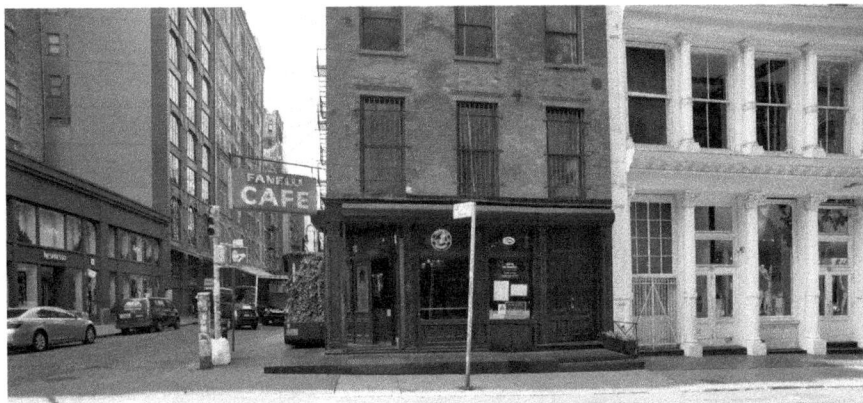

Fanelli's Café and the cast-iron building next door.

well supplied with liquor, servants and piano music, they attracted a gentlemen's clientele of businessmen, politicians and members of the upper classes. Prostitution was not a criminal offense at that time; streetwalkers could be arrested for loitering or disorderly conduct, but the expensive, relatively discreet brothels in SoHo were generally left undisturbed by the police (who probably patronized them if they could afford the high prices).

The brothels moved north in the 1870s, along with the luxury hotels, theaters and shops. (The shops are back, but the brothels, as far as we know, are not.)

On the next corner, at Spring and Mercer, one block from Fanelli's, is 101 Spring Street, an 1870 cast-iron building that was purchased by artist Donald Judd (1928–1994) in 1968 and is now owned by the Judd Foundation. Judd renovated the five-story building and used it for several years as his home and studio.

Donald Judd is a significant figure in the history of twentieth-century American art. Although he started his career as a painter, by the time Judd was in his early thirties, he had left painting behind in favor of sculpture, calling his artwork "specific objects." Using industrial materials such as metal, concrete, plywood and Plexiglas, Judd produced large architecturally influenced objects in the form of boxes and wall-mounted structures, which were the precursors of today's installations. A prolific writer and art critic, Judd believed that artwork should be installed permanently in carefully chosen environments, not temporarily situated in a museum or gallery. He

Number 101 Spring Street under scaffolding.

maintained that the relationship between an art object and the space around it is as important as the artwork itself.

Judd also believed that art—or his art—had no meaning beyond its existence; in other words, an object made of steel was an object made of steel and did not represent anything else. He was entirely opposed to representational art and did not approve of abstract expressionism, which he considered self-indulgent and sentimental.

Donald Judd was a key figure in the Minimalist art movement, although he rejected the term, and a sculptor, although he didn't call his work sculptures. He was very successful in his day and, not surprisingly, even more so after his death. His work is in major museum collections all over the world, including the Tate Modern in London and the Guggenheim and Museum of Modern Art in New York. In recent years, some of Judd's artwork has been sold at auction for many millions of dollars.

Although Judd moved out of New York in the '70s, he maintained his Spring Street studio, which the Judd Foundation is planning to open to the public as a museum.

Stewart Hitch (1940–2002) was another artist who arrived in SoHo a few years after Donald Judd. His studio was located a block or so farther along, at 85 Mercer Street. Though not as successful or, perhaps, as highly regarded as Judd, Hitch's story contains elements of mystery and tragedy.

An abstract expressionist whose work was noted for its vibrant colors and signature starburst shapes, Hitch had some success in New York before his heavy drinking took its toll. Jackson Pollock was his idol, and it appears that Hitch made a bad decision—or a series of bad decisions—by emulating Pollock's drinking and womanizing. Married and divorced three times, Hitch's third divorce cost him his loft on Mercer Street, after which he seems to have spent much of his time drinking at Fanelli's Café, where he'd apparently already been spending a lot of time.

It is what happened toward the end of his life and in the years immediately thereafter that constitutes the mystery surrounding Stewart Hitch's lost paintings. The story goes that, in the late '90s, Hitch made the acquaintance of a shady character named Ralph Iorio and agreed to become partners with him in a construction company. Having recently sold his Mercer Street loft, Hitch needed a place to store a large number of his paintings, and his new partner was happy to oblige, offering storage space in a friend's garage in Jersey City. (At this point, you are probably saying, "Uh oh.")

A year later, Hitch—who by then was terminally ill—tried to retrieve his artwork and found that Iorio had disappeared. The owner of the garage knew nothing about the storage deal, and the paintings had vanished. The location of the artwork remained a mystery at the time of Hitch's death in 2002.

Following his death, friends of Hitch pursued the quest for the missing paintings. A private detective was hired whose only discovery was that Iorio had a criminal record. The last newspaper report of the search for the artwork was published in 2003, so whether further progress has been made

Number
47 Mercer
Street.

is not clear. As of now, the whereabouts of the vanished paintings remains
an unsolved mystery.

A block or so farther down Mercer Street, at number 47, between Broome
and Grand Streets, is an 1873 cast-iron building that the *AIA Guide* calls
"lusty" (a nice adjective to describe a building). It is one of the several
locations once occupied by Alexander Roux (1813–1886).

Who was Alexander Roux? Collectors of Victorian furniture are familiar
with the name. A cabinetmaker born and trained in France, Roux arrived

in the United States in the 1830s and opened his first shop in 1836. He designed beautifully crafted, highly ornamental furniture and was taken up by the wealthy New Yorkers who favored the French Rococo style then in vogue. (Among his clients was William Backhouse Astor, a name that keeps popping up in these pages.) His furniture company, Roux & Co., had five addresses on Broadway in SoHo, as well as this five-story cast-iron building on Mercer Street, which was used as both a factory and a store.

Alexander Roux's furniture changed with the times. His company offered the public a variety of contemporary styles, but his Rococo pieces are best known today—and fetch many thousands of dollars. During the company's best years in the 1870s, Roux & Co. employed 120 craftsmen and earned half a million dollars, quite an impressive sum in those days. One of Roux's successful manufacturing practices was to employ the newly invented steam-powered saws to speed up production. This gave him time to devote to the ornate hand-carvings that characterized his furniture.

Today, Alexander Roux's furniture is in museums and private collections and appears from time to time in furniture and antique auctions. In 2007, for example, a Roux walnut sideboard with a marble top was sold for $20,350 at an estate sale.

Incidentally, the name Alexander Roux is linked with that of Louis Comfort Tiffany and Stanford White, all of whom helped furnish and decorate the interior of the Seventh Regiment Armory of the New York National Guard on Park Avenue and Sixty-sixth Street when it was built in 1877. White was only twenty-four at the time, not yet in his prime, either as an architect or as a playboy.

Not at all surprisingly, 47 Mercer Street, once the Alexander Roux store, has been converted into luxury condos.

At the very southern end of SoHo, where Mercer Street meets Canal Street, is another building that was constructed as a palace of commerce, this one for Aaron Arnold and his son-in-law, James Constable. Built in 1856–57, the Arnold Constable department store was another success story, a large, elegant shop whose staff included uniformed porters who opened carriage doors and escorted ladies into the store.

Like the other lavishly appointed department stores in SoHo—Brooks Brothers, Lord & Taylor and Tiffany's—Arnold Constable stayed for a few years and then followed the commercial migration northward, first to the Ladies' Mile (between Union Square and Twenty-fourth Street) and then onward to Fifth Avenue. When Arnold Constable finally closed its doors in 1975, its Fifth Avenue store became a local branch of the New York Public Library.

10

GREENE STREET

Architectural Masterpieces, C. Godfrey Gunther,
the Floating Subway Map and a Mural

O ur path now takes us a little farther along the back streets of SoHo. We're going to take a look at Greene Street and Wooster Street, noted more for their architectural masterpieces than for lurid tales of lust and mayhem that seem to have featured so frequently in our tour of the neighborhood.

Greene Street is, in fact, specially cited by architects and art historians for the wealth of cast-iron-front buildings that line its narrow streets. It's a pleasure to stroll the length of SoHo and enjoy the ornamental nineteenth-century cast iron, fashioned into various Grecian columns and Italianate and French Renaissance façades, as well as classical pediments and Corinthian capitals. It is amazing that so many of these palatial buildings were erected as warehouses for the larger and even grander department stores that once lined Broadway.

Two buildings in particular along Greene Street merit our attention, as much for their names as for their architecture, striking though it certainly is. These are the King and Queen of Greene Street.

The Queen, located at 28 Greene Street, between Canal and Grand Street, was built in 1873 by an architect named J.F. Duckworth, of whom very little is known (in fact, he is sometimes cited as Isaac Duckworth and sometimes as J.F.). Look all the way up to the top of the building and you'll see the elaborately decorated mansard roof, an architectural feature borrowed from the French that was very popular in New York at just the time that the Queen of Greene Street was erected. A 2011 article in the real estate section of the *New York Times* says, "The mansard mania of 1868 to 1873 swept over New York with a peculiar incandescence." (The New Era Building, which we visited on Broadway and Broome Street in Chapter 5, has a particularly fine mansard roof.)

The King of Greene Street, two blocks north of the Queen, is located at number 72, between Broome and Spring Streets, and was built by the same architect in the same year. Another cast-iron masterpiece featuring free-standing columns and a three-dimensional façade, this five-story building was originally used as a dry goods warehouse for another once-successful, now-forgotten company known as the Gardner Colby Company. You can see Colby's initials in the façade.

Like many of SoHo's cast-iron warehouses, the King and Queen of Greene Street fell on hard times after the textile industry moved away but have been saved by the New York City Landmarks Preservation Commission and restored to their original splendor. The Queen of Greene Street was awarded a New York Landmarks Conservancy Award for Preservation—also known as a "Preservation Oscar"—in 2010. In February 2012, a three-bedroom apartment in this building was listed at a monthly rental of $13,500.

On the southwest corner of Greene and Broome, half a block south of the King, is another noteworthy building, both for its architecture and for the stories associated with it. The address is 469 Broome Street. This five-story cast-iron building has an interestingly rounded corner—i.e., the façade curves around the corner of the building where Greene Street meets Broome Street. This effect was made possible by the nature of cast iron, which could be molded and fitted around the rolled glass of the windows. Above the second-floor window in this curved corner of the building is a crown, also made of cast iron, with the words "Gunther Building" clearly visible.

And who was Gunther? There are actually a couple of Gunthers who enter into our story. The first was Christian G. Von Gunther (1795–1868), a German who came to New York from Saxony in 1815. A fur dealer, Von Gunther was associated with—you guessed it—John Jacob Astor. Von Gunther established his fur business in 1820, and by mid-century his company was one of the most successful in the United States.

The name of the business was changed to C.G. Gunther's Sons (the "Von" seems to have disappeared), and in 1860, 502 Broadway, between Grand Street and Broome Street, was erected as C.G. Gunther's Sons' Store. This was one of the earliest cast-iron commercial buildings on Broadway and the building where the fourteen-year-old Houdini would launch his career a quarter of a century later. The Gunther Building on Broome Street was

Detail of the Gunther Building: name and crown. *Watercolor by Leendert van der Pool.*

The Gunther Building, 469 Broome Street.

built in 1861 for Christian Von Gunther's son William H., who took over the business. Despite its architectural elegance, 469 Broome was used as Gunther's warehouse.

Specializing in sable from Siberia, as well as ermine and mink, Gunther's was one of the only fur shops in Manhattan offering men's as well as women's fashion. The Gunther fur business lasted well into the twentieth century; a 1930s velvet, gold lamé and fox evening coat is now in the permanent collection of the Metropolitan Museum of Art.

Another member of the Gunther family—in fact, Christian Von Gunther's oldest son—was prominent in New York City politics in the 1860s. This was C. Godfrey Gunther, one-time mayor of New York.

The Civil War years were a complicated time politically, with numerous groups in conflict with one another, as well as with the Democratic political machine, Tammany Hall. Perhaps you remember Mayor Fernando Wood (from Chapter 6)? C. Godfrey Gunther ran against Wood for the office of mayor of New York in 1861. Since they were both Democrats—Gunther was the Tammany candidate, and Wood was not—the vote was split, and a

Republican, George Opdyke, was elected. It was Opdyke, you might recall, who had to handle the Draft Riots, which pretty much ended his political career. And who stepped in in 1864? C. Godfrey Gunther. He was apparently not much of a success as mayor either, but he did manage to remove the slaughterhouses and roaming cattle from the streets of New York.

Gunther was also an outspoken opponent of the establishment of a professional fire department, which was enacted by New York State law in 1865. As we mentioned in the previous chapter, New York had been served by volunteer firefighters, but we neglected to mention that the firefighting companies were also political clubs that lent muscle—both figuratively and literally—to elections, and many of them were strong backers of Tammany Hall. Not only that, but the various firefighting units were often in rivalry with one another, which tended to result in violent confrontations (sometimes during, or instead of, their firefighting duties).

Mayor Gunther was not the only mayor to have been supported by (or perhaps owe his election to?) the fire volunteers. When the bill was presented to the New York State legislature replacing the volunteer companies with a paid fire department, he fought for his constituency but was unsuccessful.

C. Godfrey Gunther served as mayor until 1865, during which time his fur business continued to prosper, and went on to make another fortune as a partner in the Brooklyn, Bath and Coney Island Railroad.

The Brooklyn, Bath and Coney Island Railroad opened in 1863, at a time when Coney Island was still a faraway seaside resort. The first hotel, the Coney Island House, opened there in 1829, followed by a number of others, including one that Gunther himself owned—the Tivoli—which was not profitable. What was, however, very profitable was the Brooklyn, Bath and Coney Island Railroad, one of several independent steam railroad companies financed by hotel owners to bring customers to their beach resorts.

Also known as "Gunther's Road," the Brooklyn, Bath and Coney Island Railroad changed its name to the Brooklyn, Bath and West End Railroad in 1885, naming itself after the West End Terminal at Coney Island. It was consolidated with other Brooklyn transportation lines at the end of the century to form the Brooklyn Rapid Transportation Corporation, which later became the BMT. We mention all this because the name "West End" will resonate with older New Yorkers who rode on the West End subway and elevated trains before the lines lost their evocative names (such as the Culver, the Sea Beach and the Brighton) to be replaced by letters of the alphabet. We still see an occasional subway train bearing the words

The corner of Prince and Greene Streets.

"West End Express," and trains still terminate in Coney Island, but the name "Gunther's Road," as indeed C. Godfrey Gunther himself, has been largely forgotten.

One more interesting note about the Gunther Building: this was the first building on Broome Street to be converted to residential lofts. This happened in 1972, when a 2,500-square-foot loft in the building sold for $15,000.

We're still on Greene Street, which was opened at the turn of the nineteenth century and is still paved with the original (mid-1800s) Belgian blocks. Belgian blocks are a little larger than cobblestones and more expensive to produce, but they provided firmer footing for horses, an advantage on these busy streets. Greene Street was named for Revolutionary War general Nathanael Greene, a trusted companion of George Washington. A military strategist, Greene was credited with ending British occupation of the southern American colonies.

Continuing north on Greene, we're going to walk past the King of Greene Street again and head for number 110. The building at this address, the thirteen-story landmarked SoHo Building, was built in 1910 and was the tallest in SoHo until 1996, when the SoHo Grand Hotel on West Broadway surpassed it.

But we suggest that you look down rather than up. The sidewalk in front of the SoHo Building features a piece of artwork that reminds us of the work of Ken Hiratsuka (Chapter 7). Entitled *Subway Map Floating on a New York Sidewalk*, it was designed by Belgian artist Françoise Schein and has been in place since 1986. Running eighty-seven feet—the length of the SoHo Building—and occupying the full twelve-foot width of the sidewalk, the map is made of concrete and steel with the subway stations illuminated from underground. Although Schein's website describes the piece as representing a "democratic urban transport system," Brooklyn and Queens are not on the map. (Would residents of the so-called outer boroughs consider this democratic?) There are other inaccuracies in the map, but it was not really created as an aid to understanding the New York subway system.

And speaking of Ken Hiratsuka, there is a lovely piece of his sculpture, also designed with his characteristic line patterns, standing outside the SoHo Building. Entitled *Tulip* (2008), his tracery of lines is carved into an irregular vertical stone that seems to be gazing down on the subway map at its feet.

The *Subway Map* was the first of Françoise Schein's many urban map installations; her artwork has been installed in Beijing, Buenos Aires and numerous European cities. The slogan of Schein's organization, Inscrire (which means inscribe) is: "To write the human rights."

Another piece of quintessentially New York artwork is located a short way from the floating subway map. This is Richard Haas's *trompe l'oeil* mural on the Greene Street side of the building at the corner of Greene and Prince Streets. Haas, a world-renowned mural painter, has transformed city walls across America. His 1975 Greene Street mural depicts an extension of the cast-iron façade of 112 Prince Street, which Haas has wrapped around the building to create a second, painted, cast-iron wall.

Haas, who was born in Wisconsin in 1936, moved to New York in 1968, planning to stay one year, and never left. He was commissioned by City Walls, which also sponsored *The Wall* on Houston Street, to create this, his first outdoor mural. In a 1989 *New York Times* article, architecture critic Paul Goldberger wrote that Haas's murals "rescue us from the ugliness of empty walls and, in so doing, transform the cityscape around them."

Unfortunately, this splendid example of public art has not been maintained. Defaced by graffiti and partially hidden by new construction, it is still visible but in a sad state of deterioration.

The Richard Haas mural on Prince Street.

Number 139 Greene Street: the longest-running restoration project in New York.

Greene Street

Crossing Greene Street and continuing north, we come to a building that has been called "the longest running restoration project in New York," an 1825 Federal-style house that was originally built for a tailor named Anthony Arnoux. A one-family brick house, 139 Greene Street is a bit of an anomaly on this historic stretch of cast-iron buildings. But it predates much of the rest of the neighborhood and has survived the ups and downs of SoHo.

The Arnoux family apparently lived here for thirty-five years, after which 139 Greene Street became one of a number of brothels that lined Greene Street (like Mercer Street). Toward the end of the century, Greene Street became the center of New York's millinery trade, and number 139 was occupied by hatters. Later, like a lot of SoHo, the building was used for small industry. It gradually deteriorated and was cited as unsafe by the New York Department of Buildings in 1939.

When 139 Greene Street was purchased in 1974, the long and slow restoration process began. The current *AIA Guide* says that 139 Greene is "in a state of renovation without end."

Incidentally, a nice feature of 139 Greene Street is the marble trim around the doorway and window frames. Marble was a popular building material in the 1820s because of its availability; it was cut by convicts at Sing Sing Prison and sold inexpensively to the building trade.

Since we've made it to the corner of Greene and Houston Streets, we should certainly take a look at the thirty-six-foot-high Picasso statue of Sylvette, one of the (many) women in his life. It was installed in 1970, right across Houston Street in NYU's University Village. Entitled *Portrait of Sylvette*, it is an enlargement of the original, much smaller, stone sculpture. The Sylvette we are looking at weighs sixty tons, so it probably isn't going anywhere too soon.

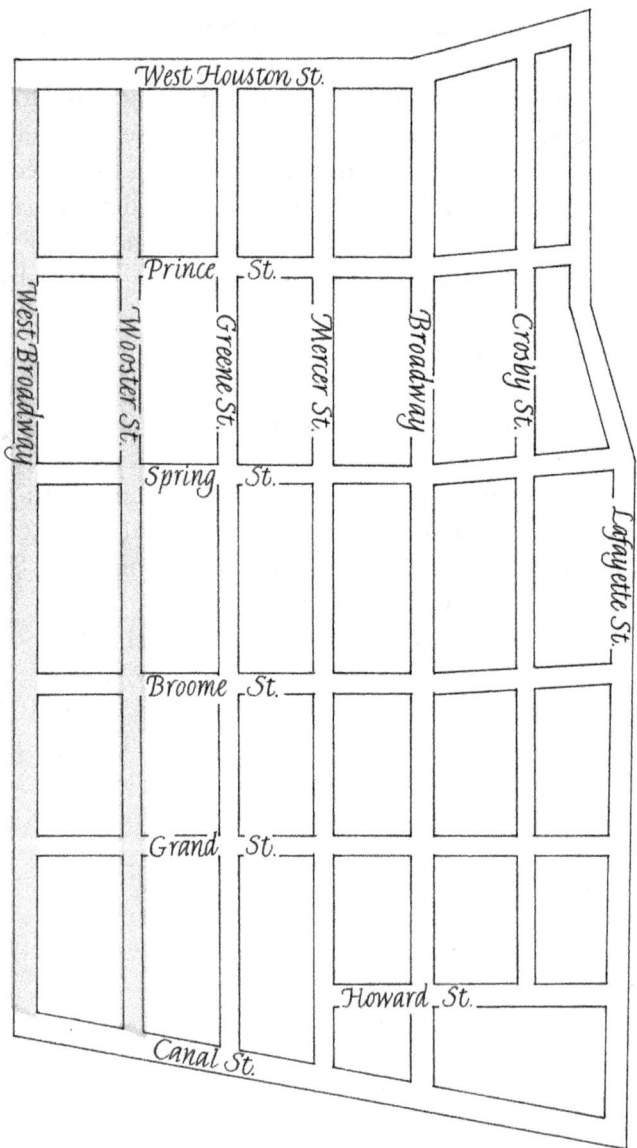

West Houston St.

West Broadway

Wooster St.

Prince St.

Greene St.

Mercer St.

Broadway

Crosby St.

Spring St.

Lafayette St.

Broome St.

Grand St.

Howard St.

Canal St.

II

WOOSTER STREET

Maciunas and the Fluxhouse, Dionysus, *Spalding Gray and the Ghosts of West Broadway*

A nd now let's go around the corner to Wooster Street, which runs parallel to Greene. David Wooster (1711–77), whose name the street bears, was yet another Revolutionary War general, but not one of the illustrious ones.

We mentioned a few pages back that in 1972, 469 Broome was the first building on Broome Street to be converted into residential lofts. In fact, 80 Wooster Street, between Spring and Broome Streets, was the very first building in SoHo to be occupied by the artists who transformed the neighborhood from an industrial wasteland to a thriving artists' community. It was George Maciunas (1931–78), a larger-than-life figure, who was central to this transformation, purchasing this seven-story warehouse in 1967 for members of the somewhat radical artistic movement known as Fluxus.

Maciunas was an artist and designer at the forefront of New York's iconoclastic avant-garde art/music/theater/film world in the late 1960s. He purchased the building on Wooster Street, which he named the Fluxhouse Cooperative, a few years before the enactment of the 1971 law that legalized the residential use of lofts. Operating without permits, Maciunas and his fellow artists did their own conversions in order to make 80 Wooster Street at least basically habitable, and Maciunas then sold the fifty- by one-hundred-foot floor-through lofts for a few thousand dollars to members of the Fluxus Group.

Following the acquisition of 80 Wooster, Maciunas purchased several other SoHo buildings and established them as artists' cooperatives, buying and converting them on a very small budget, one step ahead of city officials and the state district attorney's office.

Among the occupants of the Fluxhouse was the Film Makers Cinematheque, created by avant-garde filmmaker Jonas Mekas, born in 1922 in Lithuania and still going strong. In fact, in 2007, at the age of eighty-five, Mekas completed a series of 365 short films, which he showed on the Internet, one per day, for a year.

Another early resident of 80 Wooster Street was the Ontological-Hysteric Theater Company, founded in 1968 by playwright and director Richard Foreman. The author of more than fifty plays, Foreman, like Mekas, is an avant-garde master who has received countless awards and honors and continues to produce his plays with the Ontological-Hysteric Theater Company. His plays often have intriguing titles, such as *Deep Trance Behavior in Potatoland*, which was produced in 2008. The theater is now located two blocks south of Canal Street, at 260 West Broadway.

Maciunas, who died young, surrounded himself with New York's cutting-edge artists and performers and seems to have held them together during those wild years of the 1960s. All kinds of people were associated with the Fluxus movement: Yoko Ono, John Cage, Christo, Nam June Paik and dozens more. Here's what Maciunas wrote in his 1963 *Fluxus Manifesto*: "Purge the world of dead art, imitation, artificial art, abstract art, illusionistic art...Promote a revolutionary flood and tide in art, promote living art, anti-art, promote non art reality to be grasped by all peoples, not only critics, dilettantes and professionals."

Fluxus itself isn't easy to characterize. It has been called neo-Dada, conceptual, anarchic, subversive and certainly anti-establishment, but it laid the groundwork for much of what followed, both in terms of the New York "scene" and the settlement of SoHo by young artists in the late '60s and early '70s.

It's hard to miss the building that occupies the northwest corner of Wooster and Broome Streets, half a block south of what was once the Fluxhouse. The address is 484 Broome, and it is a massive brownstone-and-brick fortress-like structure, decorated with serpents, gargoyles, arches and towers—very imposing indeed. Although it does not have a cast-iron façade, it is considered a standout in the neighborhood; the *AIA Guide* calls it "one of SoHo's stars."

Number 484 Broome Street was built in 1895 by a Prussian-born architect, Alfred Zucker, who was responsible for a number of SoHo warehouse buildings, as well as the Charles Broadway Rouss Store on Broadway. A

Number 484 Broome Street.

successful New York architect, he left the country for Montevideo, Uruguay, rather suddenly in 1904 after his partner filed a $100,000 lawsuit, charging him with fraud. He turned up later in Buenos Aires, where he launched a second successful career that included the design of the Buenos Aires Plaza Hotel, the first in Argentina to have elevators and central steam heating. He never returned to the United States. The grand old hotel is still standing and is now a Marriott.

While we are here, we should pause for a moment at the Drawing Center at 35 Wooster, between Broome and Grand Streets. The Drawing Center has been around since 1977 and is noted for being the only fine arts institution in the country that, as its name indicates, exhibits only drawings. This small museum has a very big reputation both as a center for historical and classic artwork (drawings by Michelangelo and Turner have been shown here) and as a showcase for new artists.

Across the street from the Drawing Center is its auxiliary space, nicely named the Drawing Room. Plans are underway to expand the main exhibition space at 35 Wooster, which currently measures 2,500 square feet, smaller than some of the luxury condos in the neighborhood.

Detail of 484 Broome Street. *Watercolor by Leendert van der Pool.*

Before we leave Wooster Street, we should stop at 33 Wooster, the Performing Garage, an off-off-Broadway theater that has played an important role in New York theatrical history.

The Performing Garage was acquired in 1968 by Richard Schechter, the founder and director of an experimental theater company known as the Performance Group. Actually, the building was never used as a garage at all; 33 Wooster was a metal-stamping and flatware factory before it was transformed into a theater.

The Performance Group developed and produced new theatrical works there for thirteen years, the very first of which was Schechter's somewhat

Number 33 Wooster Street, the Performing Garage.

notorious—and most definitely memorable—*Dionysus in 1969.* Based on Euripedes' *The Baccae, Dionysus in 1969* was an avant-garde play that blurred the distinction between audience and performers. (Those of us who were around in the '60s probably remember *Dionysus in 1969* as the show in which not only did the actors take off all their clothes, but members of the audience did as well! There was much more to it than that, but somehow that detail is hard to forget.)

After Schechter resigned in 1980, the Performing Garage became home to another theater company: the Wooster Group. In fact, the Performance Group and the Wooster Group overlapped for a few years, both in terms of chronology and membership. The Wooster Group, which has presented its works at the Performing Garage for nearly forty years, now owns the building and is part of the Grand Street Artists Co-op, which was originally part of the Fluxus movement, another of the many links that exist within SoHo.

The Wooster Group was co-founded by Elizabeth LeCompte, who has directed all of its production since 1975, and Spalding Gray (1941–2004). Gray, who wrote and performed autobiographical monologues, had a busy and successful career in the theater, the cinema and on television but ended his life sadly and somewhat mysteriously. A victim of depression, Gray disappeared one night in the winter of 2004 after phoning home from the Staten Island Ferry terminal. His body was discovered two months later in the East River; it has been assumed that he jumped from the Staten Island Ferry. His legacy includes four films of his performance pieces, including the well-known *Swimming to Cambodia* (1987) and *Monster in a Box* (1991), and the posthumously released *And Everything Is Going Fine*, a documentary directed by Steven Soderbergh (2010).

In recent years, the Wooster Group, while still officially at home at the Performing Garage, performs worldwide, with recent scheduling including shows in London and Stratford-on-Avon. It is in residence three months per year at the Baryshnikov Art Center on West Thirty-seventh Street.

The final leg of our journey around SoHo will take us to West Broadway, which, after Broadway itself, is probably the first street that comes to mind when we think of SoHo, especially when we think of SoHo during its cultural renaissance in the 1970s.

But before we say hello and goodbye to the West Broadway gallery scene, let's look at the street itself.

Prior to 1870, West Broadway was called Laurens Street, after Henry Laurens, a politician and statesman from South Carolina who served as president of the Continental Congress from 1777 to 1778. (Laurens later spent fifteen months as a prisoner in the Tower of London and was freed in exchange for British general Charles Cornwallis in 1781. But that's a tale for another day.)

In 1870, the street was widened and renamed South Fifth Avenue, a name that lasted less than thirty years. During that period, buildings were numbered from north to south, starting at Washington Square in Greenwich Village. When the name was changed from Laurens Street to West Broadway in 1899, the buildings were renumbered, starting on Canal Street and heading north. You can still see some irregularities; for example, 383 West Broadway has the number 159 on its façade—that would have been 159 South Fifth Avenue.

Much of West Broadway is lined with cast-iron warehouses, now mostly converted to residences, built in the last quarter of the nineteenth century. An exception is an 1885 brick and stone building located just off West Broadway on Spring Street, heading in the direction of Thompson Street, that once housed the electric works of the Sixth Avenue Elevated Railroad, which traveled along (above) West Broadway between 1872 and 1938.

A loading platform at West Broadway and Broome Street.

A couple blocks south, at 310 West Broadway, between Grand and Canal Streets, we find the SoHo Grand Hotel, built in 1996, the tallest, if not the most attractive, building in the neighborhood. The first hotel to be built in SoHo in over one hundred years, the SoHo Grand was soon followed by others as more and more tourists arrived, attracted by the shops and restaurants that line these popular streets.

Many years before the SoHo Grand Hotel appeared on West Broadway, the Church of St. Alphonsus Liguori occupied this corner of the street. It was built in 1870 for a German-Catholic Redemptorist congregation. Unbeknownst to the builders, the church was erected over a hidden (and apparently forgotten) underground stream and eventually started to sink into the streambed. The church and the nearby rectory and church hall were all deemed unsafe and demolished in 1980.

The Church of St. Alphonsus Liguori left its mark on New York City history when labor leader Frank Tannenbaum (1893–1969) and 189 unemployed workers occupied the church in a 1914 demonstration. Tannenbaum, representing the Industrial Workers of the World, was arrested (along with all 189 other demonstrators) and charged with inciting to riot, for which he served a one-year term at Blackwell's Island prison. He later had a distinguished career as a scholar, writer and professor of criminology at Cornell University and of Latin American history at Columbia University. His invasion of St. Alphonsus Liguori Church was described in Emma Goldman's 1931 autobiography. (Emma Goldman—anarchist, trade union advocate, feminist and free-speech activist—also served a year on Blackwell's Island, though not at the same time.)

Before we leave West Broadway, we should make a stop at one of SoHo's many ghost locations: 420 West Broadway. At one time, not so many years ago, this was a major center of contemporary art, with world-renowned galleries that featured the newest and hottest artists. A former paper warehouse built in 1892, the building was acquired in 1971 by art dealers Andre Emmerich and Leo Castelli in partnership with the owners of a company called Hague Art Deliveries, located on West 108th Street, where Castelli and Emmerich rented storage space.

SoHo was most definitely not a prime location (for anything) in those days, but when the building on 108th Street was scheduled for demolition, the three partners took a big risk and purchased 420 Broadway. Emmerich, Castelli and Castelli's ex-wife, Ileana Sonnabend, each opened a gallery and were apparently quite surprised when twelve thousand people showed up at the first opening.

What followed is now part of American art history. The building housed a number of important galleries over the next two decades, specializing in all that was cutting-edge. (You may have heard of the 1972 "Seedbed" exhibition that took place in the Sonnabend Gallery. Modesty prevents us from describing it.) As more and more galleries opened—in this building and on the adjacent streets—SoHo became the epicenter of the contemporary art world.

But it was not to last very long. As we mentioned in Chapter 2, the turnover from art center to shopping center was rapid. The Andre Emmerich Gallery moved uptown in 1979, followed by Mary Boone (another major gallery), who left in 1984. By the late 1990s, Sonnabend had moved to Chelsea, and Leo Castelli closed his SoHo gallery shortly thereafter.

In 1997, 420 West Broadway was put on the market; it reopened a few years later, transformed into luxury co-ops. Somehow, the price of $13,900,000 for a loft (OK, a large loft) no longer shocks us. Perhaps the current residents of the building are hoping to see the ghosts of Andy Warhol, Jasper Johns and Donald Judd roaming the hallways.

Number 420 West Broadway.

There are still a number of galleries in SoHo, though only a few are on West Broadway. One of the pioneers, O.K. Harris, is still at 383 West Broadway (159 South Fifth Avenue). In fact, that gallery has been there since the late 1960s, predating the opening of 420 West Broadway by several years.

One other tale about 420 West Broadway is about dance rather than fine art, and it's a lovely final image with which to conclude our tour of SoHo.

In 1973, the roof of 420 West Broadway was the stage for a performance by the Trish Brown Dance Company. More accurately, it was part of the stage. The dance, entitled *Roof Piece,* was choreographed by Trish Brown and performed by fifteen members of her modern dance company, who formed a half-mile-long chain of dancers on rooftops extending from 35 White Street in Tribeca to 420 West Broadway. Viewers, who were happily observing from nearby rooftops, watched as waves of movement appeared to ripple from dancer to dancer, ending with Brown herself on the roof of 420 West Broadway.

Roof Piece was first performed in 1971 a few blocks east, on roofs stretching from Wooster Street to Lafayette Street, and has recently celebrated its fortieth anniversary with a show on the High Line.

If SoHo is populated with ghosts, it's nice to imagine some of them dancing in a chain along the rooftops.

Index

About the Authors

A LFRED POMMER of New York City is a self-employed licensed New York City guide. He has been giving private and publicly scheduled neighborhood walking tours for groups or individuals in Manhattan's many diverse neighborhoods for over twenty years. During that time, Alfred has been constantly researching and improving each tour. He retired in 1991 after twenty-five years of service with the New York City Parks Department. During that time, he attended college part time, eventually graduating with a degree in labor studies. Alfred has had several articles about the history of various locations, streets and neighborhoods in Manhattan published by *10003 Magazine*.

A native of Brooklyn, New York, ELEANOR WINTERS has been exploring New York City on foot for several decades. A commercial and fine artist specializing in calligraphy, she has written five books for calligraphers, all of which are currently in print. Eleanor lives half the year in Brooklyn and half in Paris and teaches calligraphy to beginners, as well as professionals, in Europe and the United States. She exhibits her artwork widely and is represented by the Franklin 54 Gallery + Projects in Manhattan. Eleanor has a master of arts degree from New York University.

Exploring New York's SoHo is the second collaboration by the authors. Their previous book, *Exploring the Original West Village*, was published by The History Press in 2011.

Visit us at
www.historypress.net

www.ingramcontent.com/pod-product-compliance
Lightning Source LLC
Chambersburg PA
CBHW070351100426
42812CB00005B/1484